The MIRACLE CHASE

keep the faith!
Katie

The
MIRACLE
CHASE

THREE WOMEN, THREE MIRACLES,
and a
TEN YEAR JOURNEY *of* DISCOVERY AND FRIENDSHIP

JOAN LUISE HILL | KATIE MAHON | MARY BETH PHILLIPS, PhD

STERLING ETHOS
New York

STERLING ETHOS
New York

An Imprint of Sterling Publishing
387 Park Avenue South
New York, NY 10016

STERLING ETHOS and the distinctive Sterling logo are registered trademarks
of Sterling Publishing Co., Inc.

ISBN 978-1-4027-7765-3 (hardcover)
ISBN 978-1-4027-9545-9 (paperback)
ISBN 978-1-4027-8327-2 (ebook)

Library of Congress Cataloging-in-Publication Data
Hill, Joan Luise.
The miracle chase : three women, three miracles, and a ten year journey of discovery and friendship / Joan
Luise Hill, Katie Mahon, Mary Beth Phillips, PhD.
p. cm.
Includes bibliographical references.
ISBN 978-1-4027-7765-3 (hc-trade cloth : alk. paper) 1. Miracles. 2. Hill, Joan Luise. 3. Mahon,
Katie. 4. Phillips, Mary Beth. 5. Catholic women--Religious life. I. Mahon, Katie. II. Phillips, Mary
Beth. III. Title.
BT97.3.H56 2010
202'.117—dc22

2010010656

Distributed in Canada by Sterling Publishing
c/o Canadian Manda Group, 165 Dufferin Street
Toronto, Ontario, Canada M6K 3H6
Distributed in the United Kingdom by GMC Distribution Services
Castle Place, 166 High Street, Lewes, East Sussex, England BN7 1XU
Distributed in Australia by Capricorn Link (Australia) Pty. Ltd.
P.O. Box 704, Windsor, NSW 2756, Australia

For information about custom editions, special sales, and premium and corporate purchases, please contact
Sterling Special Sales at 800-805-5489 or specialsales@sterlingpublishing.com.

Manufactured in the United States of America

2 4 6 8 10 9 7 5 3 1

www.sterlingpublishing.com

To my husband, Gene, for his encouragement,
My children, David, Alyssa, and Greg for their inspiration,
And my family and friends for their love.
—JLH

To Dick and Janie, who gave me the gift of faith
To Jim, Laura, and Allie who bring me joy at every turn.
—KM

To Liz, Andrew, and Daniel
My three greatest Miracles.
—MBP

CONTENTS

$\mathcal{P}$ROLOGUE

Miracles seem to me to rest not so much upon faces
or voices or healing power coming suddenly near us from afar off,
but upon our perceptions being made finer,
so that for a moment our eyes see and our ears can hear
what there is about us always.

—WILLA CATHER, DEATH COMES FOR THE ARCHBISHOP

JOAN

What would make three women set off in search of the Holy Grail? I hope you believe me when I tell you that it was a miracle—three miracles, to be exact.

When one of your children is teetering on the edge of death, it changes things. You are forced to cut to the chase; how you feel, what you believe, and what is important become instantly clear. When a death sentence was handed to my fourteen-year-old son, it seemed unthinkable to connect the dots and see the picture the doctors were presenting, but I had to quickly grasp the enormity of the situation in order to go on.

As I look back, I realize my family's traumatic experience in the fall became the tipping point for my life and in the lives of my two friends Katie and Meb. It caused a sudden shift in the natural order of things. As Meb later said, we were "broken open"—we discovered a new dimension to our friendship, but it changed all three of us forever.

Still, in the beginning, I wanted life to get back to normal. Once the crisis with my son had passed, Meb, Katie, and I were finally able to meet for coffee one morning. As we traded updates on our work, kids, and various activities, Katie raised her eyebrows, smiled, and asked what should have been a simple question:

"So, Joan, how are you?"

Her inquisitive manner let me know she wasn't about to let me off with the standard, a simple "I'm fine." I knew she wasn't just asking out of courtesy, like the cashier at the grocery store. Katie really wanted to know how I felt about what had happened with my son and the events that still seemed so surreal. But I wanted no part of a deep, dark discussion—I just wanted to sip my coffee in peace, relieved to know we had all survived.

"I'm fine. Really good, actually."

Katie was not convinced. She persisted. "I mean, how do you *really* feel about what happened?"

I did what I usually do when asked something I would rather avoid: I stalled. "Uh, what part, Katie?"

Not letting me off the hook so easily, her response cut to the chase. "Joan, come on: the surgery, the movie, all of it, surely—"

I knew I was in trouble when Meb interrupted in her soothing psychoanalyst voice, a voice that makes you feel calm but isn't the one she usually uses with her friends. "Isn't it possible there was a little more going on than just medical science and bizarre coincidence?"

With the Katie–Meb tag team in full swing, I knew I couldn't run away and hide; it would be best to just come clean. I looked at my two friends and told them something I hated to admit, even though it was the truth: "I don't know."

As the Chinese proverb says, "A journey of a thousand miles begins with a single step." In our case, it began with mine. If you're familiar with Lake Wobegon, the idyllic spot "where all the women are good-looking, all the men are strong, and all the children are above average"—though the three of us accepted this reputation with amusement—you have a pretty good idea of the town where we all lived, just east of San Francisco.

Katie and Meb were two of my closest friends, though they barely knew each other. Meb's oldest son, Andrew, shared sports teams with my son David, and we had spent hours on the sidelines—supposedly watching games, but mostly just talking. Truth is, I had heard of Meb long before I met her; as they say, her reputation preceded her. She was a small-town celebrity for all the work she had done in child-abuse prevention—and had even been on *Oprah*! Most people seemed to hold Meb in awe, but were also intimidated by her. I thought it was a little bit sad; she seemed to have lots of admirers, but few friends. To me, Meb was the perfect combination: she was smart and creative, and she enjoyed decorating for the holidays almost as much as I did.

I knew Katie because our daughters, Allie and Alyssa, had forged a close friendship as classmates in first grade. By the time they were ten, the girls collectively decided that Katie and I should teach their weekly religion class together. Katie was all I had wanted to be as an adolescent: tall, blond, blue-eyed, with a riveting sense of humor. As an added bonus, she loved chocolate and french fries, two of my major food groups. I admired how comfortable Katie seemed to be in her own skin: she was self-confident and tenacious. While I could waffle upon occasion, Katie was sure of herself, hanging on to her convictions like a dog with a bone. She seemed to be fearless.

I love putting people and projects together, and had tried to introduce these two wonderful women before. I had hoped the three of us could launch a new venture—something to keep us engaged and make the world a better place. After all, we had skills and interests that complemented each other. Katie approached life as the straightforward banker she was: "The bottom line . . ." usually crept into her conversations, preceding some quickly deduced, eminently logical conclusion. Meb, on the other hand, was pure intuition, a psychotherapist who routinely thought outside the box, flexible in her thinking and willing to appreciate the value of spiritual alternatives. I was used to dealing with strong personalities and finding common ground after twenty-five years as a healthcare executive. Ambitious and optimistic, the three of us wanted it all: career, family, home, and happiness ever after.

Katie, Meb, and I also shared the same religion—or, more accurately, we shared the same childhood religion. Our uniformed Catholic schooling, shrouded in mystery and Latin mumbo-jumbo, had given way to Jesuit colleges where questioning and intellectual pursuits were embraced. For the first time in our lives, practicing our faith became optional, and each of us had, by varying degrees, exercised our freedom to opt out. We harbored doubts, sometimes acting as believers, sometimes even believing that we were. But years went by quickly, and, for the most part, any hint of the miraculous went unnoticed—our lives became so busy that there was barely time to think, much less to think about God.

By 1999, we had built up decades of cynicism along with a more adult perspective about the religious indoctrination of our youth. The pretty pictures of winged angels and a benevolent white-bearded God gave way to a smorgasbord of religious remnants, each of us clinging to something different from our search for who or what God really was.

When I was a child, a favorite aunt had given me a book and record album of the story of St. Bernadette, a sickly, destitute fourteen-year-old girl living near Lourdes, France in the nineteenth century who experienced apparitions of Mary, the mother of Jesus. I never tired of the story of how, at Mary's request, Bernadette began digging in a grotto near her home, where a spring arose from beneath the dust and the dirt. Almost immediately, miraculous healings began to take place there. Although Bernadette was ridiculed and ruthlessly questioned, she remained true to her experience of the beautiful woman who had appeared to her, seemingly from nowhere. Her courage, in spite of the powerful pressure exerted by others, resonated with my own independent spirit and ignited my passion for medicine. Meb understood and shared my devotion to Mary. Katie, our resident skeptic, was suspicious where Mary and the saints were concerned, but she humored us and turned a (somewhat) tolerant ear to our conversations. Although Katie couldn't relate to my affinity for Mary, as linear thinkers we were kindred spirits— we laughed about our childhood love for paint-by-number kits and connect-the-dot pictures. Together, Meb, Katie and I represented the full spectrum of belief in the impossible: dedicated believer; committed skeptic; and me, trying hard to mediate between belief and uncertainty.

As my "I don't know" hung in the air in the coffee shop that morning, the glance I caught between Meb and Katie was one you might see when two people share a deep secret. The miraculous survival of Meb's daughter was never far from our thoughts, but I knew I had touched a different nerve, because Katie said simply, "I have a story."

The tale that Katie shared, of near-tragedy and her own survival, eclipsed even the brilliant California sunshine that day. If she was trying to jar me out of my complacency, her strategy was a success. I knew that David was alive and well, even though by all accounts he shouldn't be; still, my inclination had been to let it be and move on. But over time, Katie and Meb had come to acknowledge divine intervention in their lives and had developed the wisdom to understand that something more was at work. My two friends recognized long before I did that a miracle had occurred in my life as well.

Although I tried to seem calm, I was struggling with unanswered questions. How could I have experienced a personal miracle in today's world? Wasn't that something that only happened in the Bible or to someone else? Then one day, while driving my five-year-old son, Gregory, to the park, I had an epiphany. "Look, Mom," he said, pointing excitedly to the sky. "There's a white rainbow!"

My pragmatic side responded easily. "No, buddy, it's just the trail from a jet airplane."

"Not to me," he replied simply. "It's beautiful."

All of a sudden, I got it. Why couldn't a rainbow be white? Maybe it was time to shift my thinking. Perhaps there are "rainbows" all around us; but since we only see them a piece at a time, we mistake them for something else. Miracles happen. We may not always notice them, but they exist, and the choice to recognize a miracle is up to each of us.

We have come a long way from Katie's tongue-in-cheek query "If a miracle happens in the forest and no one is around, is it still a miracle?"

Meb's question "What if the miracle you get isn't the one you ask for?" challenged us.

And I wondered just how many coincidences it would take before I would relinquish the illusion of control, acknowledge divine intervention, and accept the idea of trust in God.

Our miracle experiences created an irreversible change in perspective. Once we accepted that miracles happened in our own lives, we couldn't go on pretending that we had an arm's-length relationship with God. Initially, Katie had the narrowest view about miracles. Her limited view fueled the fire of her skepticism. She would tell you that she was spiritually stuck in a quagmire, a skeptic who believed. Over time, Katie's view mellowed and broadened, making her escape possible. In some ways, Meb was the opposite. Her vision was big and open: in her mind, miracles could be magnanimous or could be found in everyday coincidence. She saw a miracle unfold each day in the survival of her daughter. She was a tireless advocate and drove herself and her family hard, walking a tightrope while balancing her multiple roles. Having made a deathbed promise, she was bound to keep it. Meb had jumped onto the Miracle Bandwagon early, but tried relentlessly to control the direction it would take. She was finding out that control doesn't work with miracles—they must unfold in their own way and in their own time.

The Miracle Chase became our passion, and the interaction among the three of us became the essence of our journey. We set out to answer the questions that plagued us: Why do some people get miracles and others don't? What do the voices of history and cultural traditions tell us? How can anyone believe in miracles in an age of science? And the most elusive question of all: What *is* a miracle, anyway? With our individual stories to tell and some incomplete ideas about miracles, each of us headed off in search of answers, coming together to share what we learned and then setting out again and again. We wanted to know "why," as if God would open up His playbook for us in a way He had never done for anyone else. We were explorers, peering through a telescope and able to focus a bit more clearly with each look; but in matters divine, we knew our vision would never be perfectly clear.

Our journey of the soul, which would last a decade, has been full of surprises, coincidences, and reawakenings. We never thought we would become miracle-chasers, and we are the first to admit that we haven't ended up where we thought we would when we opened our hearts to each other that day so long ago. God never did open up His playbook for us, but we forged ahead anyway, knowing that to ignore the extraordinary has its own set of consequences. As you will see in the real-life stories that follow, three are better than one to ponder and philosophize, to be passionate and fearless as we face the future—it's just too hard for anyone to shoulder alone.

Part One

CHASING MIRACLES

People fear miracles because they fear being changed—
though ignoring them will change you also.

—LEIF ENGER

❧ 1 ❧

TELLING STORIES

No miracle happens without a witness.
Someone to declare, here's what I saw.
Here's how it went. Make of it what you will.

—LEIF ENGER, PEACE LIKE A RIVER

MEB

Blind Faith

Who knows how many miracles happen on any given day in this world of ours? It is certainly something I think about more, now that I have experienced one. If trauma can ripple through the life of an individual, a family, or a community—even through time—then so, too, can the effects of the miraculous. Like throwing a rock into the middle of a quiet lake, energy ripples outward in ever-widening waves until lake meets land and the force of the wave washes onto the beach, dispersing its energy onto the shore. With a miracle, the wave ripples outward, adding amplitude and force until it returns to the shores of the eternal.

Do you believe in miracles? When I was young, I didn't give much thought to them, outside the stories of the Old and New Testaments or those on the holy cards we collected and traded like my brothers' baseball cards. Today, I have an entirely different feeling about miracles, inspiring an entirely different view of God and, certainly, a different understanding of the meaning of my life. I have come to believe that we have a duty to share our personal stories of miracles with others, allowing God's intervention into our ordinary lives to ripple outward.

My family's miracle begins in the midst of sudden shock, pain, and trauma. Elizabeth Valentine Phillips, my first baby, is six months old at the time, and I am a graduate student in Clinical Psychology enrolled in a three-hour afternoon course. My regular baby-sitter has gone home for the summer, so I take our neighbor up on her offer to share her nanny. After a morning spent checking things out, I head for school leaving Elizabeth at my neighbor's house playing on the white shag carpet. Just after five o'clock, I arrive back at the house and am surprised to see my neighbor home from work early. She tells me there's been a "little accident" and my baby has been taken to the closest hospital. I arrive at the hospital in a daze, but they tell me Elizabeth was too injured for them to treat there and she's been transferred to Children's Hospital. By the time I find out where she is, meet up with my husband, Bob, and am allowed to see her, Elizabeth is in the ICU with needles and tubes entering and exiting her fragile body. She is in a coma, paralyzed on the right side of her body and having seizures. The doctors think Elizabeth might well die, or else she will live out her life as a severely brain-damaged person (as they put it, "a vegetable").

"Her injuries are equivalent to having been thrown out of a second-story window onto concrete," one doctor tells us.

As I desperately pray for Elizabeth's full recovery, a part of me knows the unthinkable has happened and there will be no way out. Confused and in shock, Bob and I have no idea why our healthy baby is now at death's door.

I am in a place I never thought I'd be, but this is now my life, a twilight zone, where hope hangs between life and the very real possibility of death. Time becomes meaningless.

The intensive care unit where Elizabeth is being treated is very mechanical and "other-worldly." People come and go and come and go, as if we are ghosts, and we stay, and stay, and pray, awaiting some good news that will set us free. Bob and I take turns sleeping on a cot that someone put next to the bed, or occasionally on the bed in the isolation unit. Friends come to see us, one of them being so affected by the pale infant swaddled under white sheets that she faints and ends up on the bed in the isolation unit herself.

Then one lonely, desperate night, unable to sleep, I am holding Elizabeth in my arms, rocking her in the lone rocking chair that sits in the center of the unit. I find myself in a one-way conversation with my infant daughter.

It's about two A.M. and I am holding you, Elizabeth. The intensive care unit is eerie this time of night. It is definitely not quiet—the machines and monitors and tubes and tanks are on, humming and beeping away. The flashing digital lights and numbers that keep track of the lives around us cast a green glow on the walls. This is a very mechanical nursery, Elizabeth. I don't know how any of you babies sleep here.

The good news is that the nurses are busy; they are leaving us alone for a change. I can even hold you, look at your face, smell you. Just yesterday, they wouldn't let me hold you. That was such a cruel thing to do to a mother! I feel so helpless inside. They say I can't nurse you, so there are dozens of little bottles in the unit's refrigerator just for you. I go into a sterile empty room and pump my breast milk with a special hospital pump that sucks half my breast inside so I will be ready to nurse you again someday when you wake up.

Wake up, honey. I want you to hear me tell you again how much I love you. How much I want you back.

I pray for Elizabeth to the one heavenly body that I think will understand me. I have no confidence in God or Jesus at the moment, perhaps because I am surrounded by men in white coats and black pants, doctors and doctors-in-training, and even my husband, who all tell me they worry that I am not handling "this" well. Mary, Mother of God! You understand that no woman would handle the as-yet-unexplained coma of her first and only child well. I think of how you must have felt, helpless, grief-stricken, as you stood at the foot of the cross.

Elizabeth, you are silent and motionless in my arms. Something is very wrong. I cannot describe it. There is an absence of You. You have gone somewhere beyond the time and space I am living in. Don't go! We can get through this together. I want you to come back to us healthy and happy, just like before.

I begin to panic. Somehow, I know that something is terribly wrong. A plea for help wells up within me. O Mary, Mother of God, please intercede for me. Help me. . . . *"Remember, O most gracious Virgin Mary, that never was it known that anyone who fled to thy protection, implored your help, or sought your intercession was left unaided. . . ."* By now I am sobbing, so afraid for my unresponsive little girl. A hand reaches out, touches my shoulder, and gently stops my rocking. I look up into the face of a compassionate man who tells me, in a whisper-soft voice, to have faith.

"Mrs. Phillips, your baby is a victim of Shaken Baby Syndrome," he says. "This is when someone shakes a baby so hard that the brain is smashed back and forth against the skull, repeatedly. It causes brain damage, coma, even death. Unfortunately, I see far too much of this with catastrophic results, but trust me when I tell you, your baby is going to recover. She is going to be all right."

As he leaves, I feel a gentle peace inside me. And that night, the first miracle Elizabeth and I would share takes place. I tell Elizabeth "I love you. We are going to get through this together." I can't really explain how or why, but somehow, I feel Elizabeth "come back" to herself. I know she is back in my arms. Silently, I start to sing a hymn of praise and gratitude to Mary.

I wanted to thank this man, who had given me hope. Even though he said he was an intensive care doctor and we remained in the ICU for a week, I never see him again.

The next day, they let me nurse Elizabeth. They say "It's a good sign when a comatose baby can swallow." Our pediatrician tells us "Only Elizabeth can heal herself now. She's got to do the work. There's nothing more we can do." I think of something my mother routinely said as I was growing up: "We must work like everything depends on us and pray like everything depends on God."

I lean over and whisper in my baby's tiny ear:

> *I am here, too, Elizabeth. I can hold you and nourish you and pray for you. I can rock you and sing to you. I can help to make you strong again. We can do this together. I will never give up on you.*

We stay in the hospital for ten days. By the time we leave, Elizabeth is conscious. She is on medication to prevent seizures and she cannot move the right side of her body well. She is also totally blind. Her father and I will find out later that she has been shaken so hard that both of her retinas have detached, and that they cannot be repaired.

I become a perpetual-motion mother, taking Elizabeth to therapists and doctors, researching how to raise an infant who is blind. My graduate school is put on hold and my focus becomes helping Elizabeth recover. At the same time, we learn that in the United States, it is the state's legal system, not the victim or the victim's parents, that brings charges against a perpetrator of a crime. In fact, there is little room for parents in the criminal justice system, even when the victim is a helpless baby. It takes a very long time for the system to respond to what has happened to Elizabeth, but finally the nanny is charged with felony child abuse.

Time and again, we would go to court eager to put our tragedy behind us, only to be told over and over again that the case had been postponed. One official actually told me "It's not as if this is a very important case, Mrs. Phillips." After years of waiting, the nanny was finally convicted of child abuse, although I still wonder why it wasn't for attempted murder. Her sentence was stunning: a fine of one hundred dollars, five years' probation, and community service. And she was allowed to be a nanny again, because, in the court's opinion, "It is good to have a job when you are on probation." While putting words to paper once had brought me comfort, I developed writer's block the day the nanny's defense attorney subpoenaed my personal journal full of motherly, gushy sentimentality over my precious first-born and had it photocopied and distributed to the courtroom.

I was so busy in those early years, dealing with the aftermath of what happened on that day. Elizabeth learned to lift her head again, to roll over again, to sit up and to crawl again, just as she had before she was abused. Although she had been partially paralyzed from the damage to her brain, Elizabeth was slowly learning to move the right side of her body again. She was, however, completely and irreversibly blind.

How can I say this was a miracle? Because no one can explain how Liz, as we came to call her later, was able to overcome what happened to her—the brain damage and blindness, the violence—how she survived and then thrived. Doctors reluctantly refer to the "M" word when explaining Liz's recovery. My father used to go to church to pray every day for a miracle after Elizabeth was abused. Finally, I told him "Dad, we have a miracle already. Liz is Liz." The ripple effect of this miracle goes far beyond the single moment when I was comforted, suddenly knowing Elizabeth had come back to herself as I held her in my arms. From that baby in the hospital, who, the doctors thought would never fully recover, to the beautiful young woman she is now—how can that not be a miracle?

Miracles force you to look at coincidences and chance encounters through a different lens; but back then I wasn't actively looking at my life that way. Raising Liz in a world where people with disabilities are regularly discriminated against, and in a suburban community where pride, perfection, and parenthood are the three P's to live by, my life became a daily challenge.

I am changed by what has happened to Elizabeth. Deeply affected by the judge's decision to let the nanny become a nanny again, I resolved to find a way to prevent what had happened to us from happening to another family. But I was not thinking of what had happened as a miracle. More likely, I would have said that *Joan* was a miracle: she came into my life, providing me with empathy and perspective in an otherwise bleak existence in which the pain and frustration of fighting for Elizabeth had finally gotten to me. Joan knew I was devastated when she told me that her family would soon be moving because her husband had gotten a new job.

As she has told you, Joan is good at putting people and projects together; she really likes collecting and sharing friends. Not surprisingly, it was Joan's idea that Katie and I should meet. We did have much in common—we had even gone to the same college. Joan was sure that, together, we could create an opportunity to change the world. It must have been a little disappointing to her that at our first introduction there were no flashes of insight, no great unburdening of heart and soul between us, just pleasantries to humor our mutual friend.

I wonder what the three of us might have concocted together had circumstances been different, had life not interjected urgency into our plans and necessity into our friendship. Within weeks, there was a radical change in focus of what had begun with the three of us connecting in our comfortable social circle over sports and passions for philanthropy. The catalyst was as dramatic as this: Joan's son David didn't die.

Like being told that Liz was in a coma and might not live, Joan and her husband, Gene, experienced a parent's worst nightmare as they were handed a death sentence for their oldest son. In a heartbeat, everything took a back seat to ensuring David's survival. Their question about their upcoming move, "Where will we live next?," became eclipsed by "Who cares? Let's all just be alive."

I completely understood her terror.

The Heart of the Matter

Joan's story really starts years before we met, when David, her first-born, is having his four-year-old checkup with his pediatrician. As parents, by the time a child is four or five, most of us are pretty blasé when the doctor puts the cold stethoscope on the kid's chest and listens. This time, though, quite out of the blue, David's doctor says he thinks he hears a heart murmur. He suggests a "routine" trip to the cardiologist.

At the hospital, the cardiologist's first words reassure them. "I hear the murmur your doctor asked me to check on, and it's perfectly fine." Relief and gratitude spread as fast as wildfire in a parent's heart during these situations, but fear, Joan learns, spreads even faster. The cardiologist's next words are devastating: "I hear another sound, though, one that is serious. This one is a problem in his heart that will need surgery to correct." Joan tells me she felt like she had been sucker-punched. I know what that feels like.

"Oh, my God," Joan thinks, "this guy is serious; he actually wants to do another test to confirm whether David will need open-heart surgery." Having watched this type of surgery in the past, she knows full well what it entails and can't imagine what it would do to her small son.

While the testing equipment is being set up, Joan goes to find solace in the hospital chapel. Kneeling, she begs the Blessed Mary to save her son from this surgery. She knows it is a special day in the Catholic Church, the feast of Mary's assumption into heaven, and thinks it must be a good time to ask for a favor. Like me, Joan knows that no mother ever wishes to see her child suffer. Mary would definitely understand another mother's plea for help.

After her quick visit to the chapel, Joan returns back to David's side and glimpses the heart monitor with its vivid blue and red streaks streaming across the screen reflecting the blood rushing through his pumping heart. While the cardiologist watches the screen, Joan watches the cardiologist. She desperately needs to know what he's thinking. He grows puzzled, paces a while, consults with a colleague, and finally announces that what he was looking for isn't there. Everyone breathes a big sigh of relief.

Fast-forward nearly ten years, to an ordinary day in suburban San Francisco, where David is now in the eighth grade. Joan is at her first meeting of the Parents' Club as treasurer, a post she seriously tries to "Just Say No" to after being given the book *Women Who Do Too Much*. She has been "just saying no" for the two years David has attended this school, and is finally attending a meeting. However, Joan has only been there a few moments when one of the office assistants motions for her to leave the room. David is having chest pain and they don't know what to do.

As soon as she sees David, Joan knows immediately that something is seriously wrong. David is visibly scared to death. He tells her he has been running, racing against his own track record, and was stopped short with crushing chest pain.

Then the pain starts receding and he begins to feel a little better. He tries to reassure Joan: "No big deal, Mom, it's probably just some smog in the air or too much breakfast."

To cheer him up, she jokes back: "Good thing you're not your father—I'd think you were having a heart attack." David smiles, and the color slowly begins to return to his face.

After hearing about the hundred pushups at swim practice the day before, the on-call physician chalks up the episode to a pulled muscle. With a few days' rest, the incident will be over, he predicts.

However, life is not that simple.

You just have to love a mother's intuition. It isn't always rational or easily explained, but there is a connection that exists between mother and child. Joan knows that if she hadn't been at that meeting at the school that day, she would have been very happy to accept a simple explanation. But she was there and did see David, and her maternal instinct stays on high alert in spite of the physician's diagnosis. For the first time in fourteen years, Joan actually schedules David's annual physical exam early. The pediatrician tells her that

David looks fit and seems healthy and asks if she has any concerns or questions. "No," she answers honestly, "just that one bizarre experience of chest pain." The doctor seems torn by the incident, but the pain has only occurred once and he recalls the clean bill of health David received from the cardiologist years before. He hesitates, and then recommends another echocardiogram to put this latest incident behind them for good.

Joan tells us later that she felt really foolish taking a perfectly healthy child for a full cardiac workup, a child who holds the school record for running the mile and who has achieved top national swimming times. She is surprised that the cardiologist doesn't think she is silly as she recounts the isolated incident at school two months before. "Nothing could be seriously wrong," she thinks. "I have finally sunk to the depths of my own worst image of an overprotective, worry-wart mother. If I hadn't been at the school right at that time and seen David with my own eyes, we would not be here now. I would have asked David about his day, and he would have told me he had a pain in his chest. I would have asked if it was better, and he would have said yes, and I would have told him to let me know if it happened again . . . end of story." The cardiologist interrupts her thoughts. Although the routine test results are normal and everything looks just fine, he still wants one more test.

The ECHO tech is relieved to see that his last patient before his lunch break is a healthy, cooperative one. (It is, after all, a children's hospital, and anything is possible.) Once again, the colors on the screen change in ever-increasing rapidity. Yellow, red, blue, buzz, hiss and whoosh, it all conspires to unsettle Joan's nerves. The tech tells them that everything looks normal, but he has one last thing to check before they can leave. Suddenly, the tech steps away and a parade of doctors materializes. Joan has worked in medicine long enough to know that something is seriously wrong.

The problem is not exactly in David's heart. It lies at the origin of one of his coronary arteries. It is a rare condition, even rarer in one who is still alive. Instead of David's two coronary arteries being in the normal location, one on each side of his heart, both of David's formed on the same side, only millimeters apart. This presents a fatal problem when the major vessels fill with blood (as happens with exercise) and squeeze closed the trapped coronary artery that incorrectly runs between them. It is so serious that the problem is usually only found upon autopsy of someone who has suddenly dropped dead.

Over a period of a few weeks, the Hill family crosses the country, seeking out surgeons, procedures, and ideas to remedy the problem. They don't want a stopgap measure: they want a solution to last a lifetime. The diagnosis is confirmed by all known techniques, and on David's fourteenth birthday the doctors and David's family reach a consensus. An attempt to fix the problem through open-heart surgery is the only solution. It is clear that all athletic activity must cease forever. There is too much risk.

I remember one night when our families were having dinner together celebrating David and Liz's birthday; after dessert, with the kids off playing, Joan shared that she hated the Bible story of Abraham and Isaac as a child. Now this story, the one she hates most and understands least, seems to be happening in her own life. "How can we be sure this is the right decision?" she asks. "Where will I find the courage to take my robust son and subject him to this surgery that could kill him?" Joan feels that she is being asked to place David on some medical sacrificial altar. It's not an easy choice: They can find only two cases in which an attempt has been made to repair this type of problem. Both patients suffered cardiac arrest on the operating table. Not a good sign. The reality of the situation is difficult to comprehend.

The week before David's surgery, the surgeon tells them that moving the coronary artery to its proper position is an extremely unlikely proposition: the openings are just too close to one another and he doesn't think they can be separated. David can only be kept on the heart pump with his heart stopped for an hour, or he won't wake up the same person. The surgeon tells Joan and Gene that he will have to perform the far less advantageous cardiac bypass surgery. He can't take the time to pursue an improbable procedure and still have time to complete the second one. This is devastating news. Even with the bypass in place, there is no guarantee it will work. Yet David's current anatomy is a time bomb that can explode at any moment. There is no choice but to go forward.

At five o'clock on the morning of David's surgery, his home is eerily awake in the darkness. David's grandmother liberally douses his head in holy water from the spring at the shrine in Lourdes, which my mother had given me for Liz, and which I gave to Joan. Joan tells him the story of Bernadette. David is relieved. At this point, the possibility that his parents have lost their minds wouldn't surprise him. His first thought upon hearing that the water was from Lourdes is that it came from our local ice cream shop (Loards), and he knows for sure that the water there doesn't have any healing qualities.

Check-in, pre-op, and final hugs at Children's Hospital move quickly, and David walks bravely into the heart room for surgery, pushing his IV pole beside him, accompanied by a nurse. Joan and Gene have just settled in to the tiny operating room's waiting area, when an air of increased activity around them indicates that something unexpected is happening. A nurse notices them, and comes over to tell them: "David is anesthetized, but the equipment needed for his surgery must be used for another, more critical patient." They are sent to the main surgical waiting area to see if David's surgery will be canceled or will continue. Joan knows that as they wait, another life, someone else's child, is hanging in the balance. After a while, Joan wanders outside of the waiting room and runs into one of our neighbors, a physician in the neonatal unit. Tuning in to the sadness in his eyes, she asks about his day and is distressed when he tells her about the infant who has just died on the operating table. Joan tells him that the patient in the other operating room is her son, and they are waiting to see if his heart surgery will go forward. He promises to check on him. "Is this the way the world works?" Joan thinks. "One life goes on, while another passes on?"

Much like the room Bob and I had waited in while doctors determined whether Liz's retinas could be repaired, the surgical waiting room during David's operation is an earthly limbo, a place that fills you with a terrible vulnerability, a sense of helplessness and lack of control. Suddenly, you are forced to realize—and suffer from the knowledge—that at this moment you can do nothing to help your child. To calm the parents, there is a TV constantly tuned to talk-show central, the screen dominated by a parade of the bizarre with messages of inane relationships and experiences. After a quick glance at the TV, Joan and Gene had made themselves comfortable as far away from it as possible. That's why I have such a hard time finding them way off in the corner when I come in with sandwiches that no one wants to eat, and some Asian pears that temporarily provide a novel distraction. (No one wants to eat these either.)

A while later, when we are all hunkered down together in our safe little corner, the waiting-room volunteer comes over to find us because there is a phone call at the desk and the nurse in the operating room wants to speak to one of David's parents. Joan walks over and takes the call—she can't bear to sit still—and she finds out that David's surgery is proceeding along as planned and he is now on cardiac bypass, the most dangerous part of the operation. As she hangs up the phone, Joan hears the name "Louise, Louise," in a loud voice, coming from the television. She looks over and sees that instead of Jerry Springer, *The Song of Bernadette* is suddenly playing on the screen. The other parents in the waiting room start talking at once. They are confused and question "What just happened? Who is this Bernadette and how did the station get changed?" Joan starts to tell them the familiar story. They are intrigued, and no one wants to change the station back.

Joan is mesmerized—Luise (pronounced the same as "Louise") is her maiden name. She believes, with crystal-clear certainty, that the face of Bernadette on the screen is a message sent directly to her. In that moment, the world takes on a surreal quality. Having delivered her child to the altar of sacrifice, Joan decides to finally surrender control and place her trust in God. For the first time in this ordeal, she feels at peace as she watches Bernadette's story unfold. She tells us she is enveloped by a warm, comforting presence.

As the movie ends, the surgeon arrives with miraculous news. Though, just a week before, he had said that the optimal repair was impossible, when he looked at the beating heart from inside David's chest, the minuscule two-millimeter space between the arteries that he needed, no more than the thickness of a nickel, was there: *exactly*.

Knowing how important it had been to me that my friends came to the hospital after Elizabeth was abused, a few days later I take my son, Andrew, David's good friend, to see him in the intensive care unit. Memories come rushing back to me as I push the door open; I become nauseated, then freezing cold, then dizzy. I force myself to go in. There is David, showing off his throat-to-bellybutton bandage to Andrew. You wouldn't know that this is a boy who has just stared death in the face.

"Hey, guy," Andrew says. "How's it going?"

"Okay," says David. "The food's not so great, and," he confides, "surgery was the pits."

"I know just how you feel," says Andrew, very sincerely. "I had to have surgery once."

This is news to me.

"Yeah," Andrew continues, "I had an ingrown toenail that my dad tried to operate on—wanna see?"

This is how life goes on. I look at Joan. We laugh.

Having thanked God for having Joan in my life, I know Joan was equally thankful for having Katie and me in hers right then. She says we kept her sane, which is pretty funny to me because I am often accused of being a crazy lady about Things of Elizabeth and The Other Children. When the three of us are able to get together "for fun" again, it seems like months—not weeks—have passed. At this point, having bonded around the crisis with David, social pretenses disappear. Our conversation is that of old friends who have confronted the frailty of the human condition. Katie and I both understand that something unusual has occurred in the Hills' experience and that we are still within that delicate time frame before the mind forgets or perhaps rationalizes the circumstances away. You might say our collective soul at that moment is open. Just as Joan finishes an update on the new improved David, Katie says, simply, "I have a story." Joan and I exchange looks. I think we both knew this wasn't going to be any old story.

Deliver Us from Evil

"It was 1975, the summer after my freshman year in college. I was working in San Francisco near Union Square. I got off work at three o'clock every day, an hour before I caught the ferry home, so I always had time to kill." Katie takes a deep breath and continues. "I was window-shopping in front of I. Magnin when this guy approached me. He was maybe thirty, clean-cut, and preppy. That's the thing I've always remembered: how clean-cut he was. 'Excuse me,' he said, 'I am a stranger in town and wondered if you could help me. I need to look up a friend's parents. I've just had eye surgery and can't do the close-up work to look in the phone book. Can you please help me out?'"

Katie tells us her immediate reaction was to put to work the often-repeated message from childhood, *Don't take candy from a stranger,* and so she said she had to get going and turned to get to the crosswalk. He followed her, repeating his request as she waited for the light to change, and added that he knew the parents' last name and their street. "It would only take a minute or two." Again she demurred, and again he followed her, this time into the crosswalk as she crossed the street. "I am staying just up the street at the Hyatt. There's a phone book in the lobby. Won't you please help me out?" By now they were on the other side of the street, and he had said the magic word "lobby," a crowded spot where Katie knew she would be safe and another lesson from childhood could be put to use: *Be a good Samaritan.* Besides, she still had plenty of time to catch her ferry. Katie agreed to accompany him to the hotel.

The Hyatt in San Francisco is built on a hill, and so they entered the hotel one floor below the lobby and got into the elevator. As Katie expected, there were plenty of people around. When they reached the lobby level, everyone exited except the two of them. Katie saw then that he had pressed the button for the mezzanine floor. She started to feel uncomfortable, but she stayed where she was. Somehow, she was able to convince herself that the mezzanine would also be busy with people. But when the two of them exited the elevator, the floor was deserted.

"My mind went blank, and although I recognized that I was feeling vaguely uncomfortable, I continued to follow him," Katie explains.

"We entered a long conference room. At the far end was a pay phone attached to the wall and a phone book resting on the metal shelf below it. He stood behind me, and I began to look through the white pages for a Brown family with an address on Marina Boulevard. There were several columns to look down. A minute or two passed, maybe more.

"Suddenly, the reality of the situation hit me—not in order, or even in real time, but instantaneously. I was alone with a stranger, in an out-of-the-way area of a hotel, and no one knew I was there. Where was the evidence of this guy's eye surgery? No patch, no scar, no bandage. Why doesn't he know the first names of his friend's parents? The common name I was searching for was like searching for a needle in a haystack.

"I was terrified, animalistic terrified. I realized I had been lured onto a quiet floor into a room alone with this stranger. Exactly what I'd been taught my whole life not to do.

"I turned around in a daze. The man's face had hardened and his eyes had darkened as if he were working himself into a rage. When our eyes met, he knew that I knew I was trapped, and terrified. This seemed to be part of his plan."

I don't know about Joan, but I begin thinking "Good God, this is like a bad horror movie—I can't believe she's here telling us this."

"Suddenly," Katie goes on, "there is a movement at the door; a bellman walks in, locks eyes with mine, and says to me, in this earnest voice, 'Don't you think you should be going now?' In a daze, I accompany him out of the room and follow him as he leads me down the empty hallway and into the open door of a waiting elevator. The guy does not follow us. When I get out on the lobby level, it's like stepping back into the real world. I felt totally numb. Seconds later, I turned to thank the bellman, but he was gone.

"Days passed before I mustered the courage to tell anyone. I felt so embarrassed by my stupidity. When I finally told my mom, her response was so . . . well, Catholic. She brought me home a book about angel encounters from the local library. I tried to tell myself that the bellman's appearance was a bizarre coincidence and that the stranger didn't really want to harm me. If the bellman hadn't shown up when he did or, most importantly, said what he said, I could have explained it away. Still, I was never able to convince myself that it was just luck. No explanation ever satisfied the circumstances of his arrival. Years would go by before I told another soul about what happened that day. There were times when I would wake up in the middle of the night and think about what had happened. The bellman's words have always haunted me, along with my last look at the stranger's face."

Joan and I are stunned. We understand that this could have happened to either one of us, given the way we were brought up.

"That's not all," Katie says, as she interrupts our private reactions to her story and spells out the clincher. "Although I never forgot it, nearly fifteen years went by without any real desire on my part to figure out what happened that day. I knew it didn't add up, but I couldn't bring myself to go back to all the religious hocus-pocus. I had discarded tales of angels and devils and life everlasting a long time ago, right about the time my high school religion teacher told us girls we were 'all little Eves, born with the potential for leading boys astray.'"

We laugh in the way only Catholics can when recalling crazy childhood memories induced by well-meaning nuns. Our laughter breaks the tension, but to our surprise, Katie isn't finished with her shocking story.

"One night in early 1989, with Laura and Allie tucked into bed and asleep, Jim and I finally got around to reading the morning newspaper, the *San Francisco Chronicle*. All of a sudden, Jim looked up from the front-page section. 'My God, Katie, I think this is your guy,' he told me as he handed me the paper and pointed to the headline story and picture on the front page. There was serial killer Ted Bundy staring back at me. He had been executed in Florida. I felt the terror rise up all over again as I read the article detailing his killing spree through several states and over many years and the resemblance of his victims, who were eerily like me in every respect: nearly all between the ages of nineteen and twenty-one, five feet six or seven inches tall, thin, long blond or brown hair parted in the middle."

Feigning injury to lure his victims, combined with his clean-cut looks and persistence, were hallmarks of his early killings. He was a suspect in the murders of two young women in the Bay Area during the mid-seventies when he was at the height of his murder spree. He had a girlfriend in the area, and he was a frequent visitor to San Francisco during that time.

"By the time I finished reading every word, I felt it in the aching pit in my stomach. Jim was right. This was my guy."

It's easy for us to imagine the long, blond-haired, girl-next-doorish gal who Katie had been back then. What can you say when your friend shares the fact that she's been spared Death by Bundy? Her story is The Bombshell of Inescapable Truth that underscores the old saying "Real life is stranger than fiction."

We are, for once, all speechless.

The gauntlet had been thrown down: three women, three miracles.

Part Two

THE CHASE IS ON

". . . it is incomparably more difficult to believe
the Divine Being should do one miracle and no more,
than that He would do a thousand. . . ."

—JOHN HENRY CARDINAL NEWMAN

2

WISE GUYS

By order of the King,
God is forbidden to perform miracles in this place.

—GRAFFITI, 1732, ST. MEDARD CEMETERY, PARIS, FRANCE

JOAN

We decided then and there to try to find out all we could about miracles. It was our project—like having our very own "Miracle Club." Chasing miracles became a way to connect as friends, to heal past hurts, to resolve—and maybe even dissolve—issues with the Catholic Church, and to find meaning again in our relationship with the Divine.

When we first met, we agreed that we were not experts on religion and certainly would never become philosophers. This was neither our goal nor our nature. We were hardly reclusive intellectuals, sitting in solitude, reading, writing, and meditating on life's great mysteries: these were luxuries afforded to past generations of philosophers and scientists that clearly did not apply to us.

"I'll bet the lives of these great geniuses would have been different if they had been responsible for children, homework, housework, and family," Meb mused as she arrived late at one of our meetings, wet hair piled on her head.

After our coffeeshop experience, we decided we had to get serious if we really were going to investigate miracles and ever hope to write a book on them. My house became Miracle Central for our weekly meetings. Meb brought Bob's flipcharts from his consulting business, I scrounged up enough colored pens from our religious-education class, and the kitchen was open for coffee. Create a business plan, write a mission statement, divide up our miracle investigation among the three of us, and in a few months' time we would have our answers. Or so we naïvely thought. . . .

From the beginning, we wanted to satisfy our intellectual curiosity as well as nourish our soul. We sought answers to our burning questions and fully expected that our discoveries would bring order to the universe. It was no wonder that we had to write our own miracle book. We had a hard time finding the information we wanted. So much was either too simplistic or overly intellectual. Our flip-chart sheets full of our ideas about the miraculous were torn off and used as temporary wallpaper in the room around us; later, one of us would transcribe the sheets into our miracle meeting notes to be used as the framework for our next meeting.

"We need to tap into people's feelings of un-connectedness," Meb suggested as we developed goals and objectives at our first meeting. At one point, Meb bounded up off the couch, grabbed the red marker from my hand, and explained: "See, like this. . . ," as she constructed a Venn diagram of connectedness—targeting intellectualism, spirituality, and friendship.

We read volumes on miracles in diverse cultures, investigated an array of scientific explanations, and sought out information on paranormal activity. We kept track of our research on index cards that our children made fun of but which were a helpful way of sharing information and sources.

As the weeks passed, each of us brought fascinating information to every meeting, but we found that it was hard to zero in on exactly what questions we were trying to answer. The three of us could go from the ethereal to the mundane in a matter of nanoseconds.

I wanted to explore what the experts had to say about miracles. "Why start from scratch?" I thought. "This is like any other research project. No problem."

Katie's approach was more haphazard. She looked at myriad topics, from the concept of God to science and religion, all the while searching books for earth-shattering, life-altering "thunderbolt" miracles, as we called them. She took on the role of miracle gatekeeper, an elitist always in search of the "better" miracle.

Meb's view of miracles leaned more to the unusual than the traditional. For a long time, she was in "it's all about the journey" mode (her clinical psychology background notwithstanding). Meb explored the miraculous wherever her cursor would take her, settled in her upstairs loft (which functioned as her home office). Her impressive spiritual library surrounded her on all sides and was a testament to the number of spiritual book clubs she had joined over the years.

Our miracle chase held a heightened sense of urgency for me because, right after our crisis with David had passed, we made a family decision for Gene to take the job he had been offered in Boston, and moving day was only a few months away. My goal was simple: by the time I moved to Boston, I wanted to have learned all I could about the changing face of miracles across the centuries—to "get down to business and get this thing done." It was the one place in my life I thought I had some control.

Under the crunch of time, I felt driven. I was not convinced that a miracle had happened in my life, but I knew Katie had experienced a knock-'em-down, drag-'em-out miracle. Listening to her story was probably one of the few times in my life when I was glad I was short and dark instead of tall and blond. I was also lucky enough to understand Meb's miracle in Liz, because while we may all say that each of our children is a miracle, trust me: they exist in a very different world than the one Elizabeth inhabits. In my mind, there was no doubt that both of my friends had been affected by miracles.

Although I was really grateful for the series of coincidences that had fallen into place to save my son's life, I didn't think being at the middle school at the exact time of David's crisis had been a miracle: rather, it was just a case of being the right person in the right place at the right time. Even the fact that, for the first time in years, our school system would be closed for a week over Thanksgiving, prompting an already scheduled holiday trip back to Boston, where we were able to squeeze in cardiologist visits three thousand miles from home: no miracle there either, just good planning. *The Song of Bernadette* on TV calling out my name in the waiting room as I passed by and the feeling of peace that enveloped me actually felt closer to *The Twilight Zone* than a miracle. And the fact that the surgeon was able to perform the procedure he didn't think was possible—was that a miracle, or just plain skill? You tell me. I was torn between wanting to believe and being afraid to believe. Somehow the stars had aligned in a perfect way to ensure a happy ending to what in every other known case had meant instant death.

I was a reluctant believer. How could this series of fortuitous events have happened in my family, and why *would* it? Unlike everything else in my life, I had never felt the need to over-think the whole God thing. I was content with my shallow belief of who, or what, God really is. It never remotely crossed my mind that a miracle would get me to think about God in such a deep and personal way.

As a child of the sixties and the product of a very Catholic upbringing, I wished that the notion of "cafeteria Catholics"— selectively picking and choosing personal beliefs at a smorgasbord of doctrine—had been invented earlier. It would have spared me a lot of undue angst. Unlike Meb and Katie, I hadn't grown up in California and didn't have an Irish bone in my body. But I was close enough—a first generation Italian, raised in the suburbs of Boston. I remembered leaving the comfort of my local public school in third grade for the uncertainty of the more distant parochial one. I realized early on that even though the new school was in the next town, the short bus ride actually transported me light-years away. Real nuns in long black habits with funny hats, religion class daily and not just on Sundays—for the first time, I came face to face with the rigid, inflexible God of the catechism and the Old Testament. Good at memorization, I thrived in this environment without ever really believing that God had created us only to condemn us to eternal damnation for petty infractions, or that He required the sacrifice of our children in order to prove our devotion. Fortunately, I had little need of consistency and accepted the contradiction between what I was taught and what I believed. I reasoned that God had to be more than fire and brimstone: unconditional love simply *had* to be in His lexicon.

So off I went, searching for God somehow present within this context of love, and with full recognition that, for me, a big part of the process of chasing miracles was going to be my attempt to understand them. While I believed that miracles happen, I struggled with the idea that God would bother reaching into the lives of an individual family. I needed to know what others had learned and experienced about miracles over the ages, hoping to find some precedent for how and why one could have happened to me. It seemed logical to go back to a place where I had found answers before, a place that for me was a place of retreat, quiet, and logic—the library. The stacks and cavernous mounds of volumes of centuries of intellectual pursuit and knowledge housed there reassured me. The library was a refuge where I could be alone with my thoughts and come up with some answers. From California to New England, I collected library cards in my wallet the way some people hoard the credit cards you receive in the mail. Whether I sat at those long oak tables or the cozy study carrels, it didn't matter—I was staring into the words of many of the greatest minds the world has ever produced, finding a way around my doubts and developing a logical framework for thoughtful discussion with Katie and Meb. I wanted to prove to them that miracles were a serious matter. You couldn't say "Oh, that was a miracle" just because something good had happened. I wanted to remind them that far greater minds than ours had weighed in on miracles and been stumped by their complexity.

Searching for answers, I sought proof of my friends' convictions in the opinions of recognized experts. I wasn't very discerning about men and miracles over the ages. "The more, the merrier" was my approach. I was looking for sheer volume, seeking support for a position that suddenly was no longer the comfortable arm's-length, at-church stuff, but was, as Meb likes to say, the in-your-face kind of stuff.

I was dangling on the edge of faith, conflicted and anxious, not really understanding all that had happened, glad David had survived, but wanting to comprehend the certainty of my friends' belief. While Katie had had the luxury of taking years to come to terms with her miraculous rescue, and Meb's miracle was evolving daily, the miracle in my life had happened in real time during our relationship as friends. Though Meb and Katie called it a Miracle, I had to be convinced that the events of the past months were miraculous in the fullest and deepest meaning of the word.

The list of experts became exhaustive as well as exhausting: Aristotle, Plato, Augustine, Aquinas, Descartes, Pascal, Locke, Donne, Calvin, Hobbes, Spinoza, Newton, and Einstein—all had had something to say about miracles. Who knew? It was pretty intimidating, a veritable Who's Who of geniuses and philosophers, representing many of the greatest minds in the subjects of science, mathematics, literature, philosophy, and religion. The Smart Guys, as we initially called them, were, like us, products of their own times. They were men whose revolutionary thinking rocked their worlds. These guys didn't write much that could be called light reading, nor did they all agree. They would be rolling over in their graves at the thought of the three of us—women, no less—undertaking this charge.

Struck by the number of rational men who thought miracles were only attached to the Bible and ceased with the Apostles, it didn't make sense to me that a particular church thought miracles happened only to them and theirs. In spite of its self-serving nature, that's exactly what some of the brilliant minds of their day believed.

I thought it was ironic; these erudite men and their far-reaching advances were not so different from the three of us.

"Like the Smart Guys, I once had dreams of discovering something remarkable. In my case, it was the cure for the common cold," I admitted to Meb and Katie at one of our meetings.

"God, Joan, why shoot so low?" Meb teased.

"A really long time ago," I reminisced, "when I was looking at colleges, I had an interview with a professor and asked what I could do with a major in biology. The professor's answer always annoyed me. She said, 'Chief Justice Oliver Wendell Holmes and the novelist John Steinbeck were both biology majors. They recognized that the study of science opens up a world of possibilities, because it teaches a method for thinking.' I wanted scientific success, and I thought I was being patronized with irrelevant information."

Katie and Meb knew I had attended that college, compliments of a scholarship I couldn't pass up, majored in biology, and even had taken a course from the clueless professor. What they didn't know was that, while I confess to being pretty logical and organized, I have to admit that for much of my life I have been so busy *doing* that I often forget to take the time to *think*.

"Fortunately, Greg has already informed me that thinking is his favorite thing to do," I bragged about my youngest son. "And guess what: he even credits me with teaching him." (Thank God, I've learned as well, because thinking is a prerequisite on this road of miracle-chasing.)

As I gained a historical perspective, it became clear that the task of understanding miracles was neither easy nor risk-free. Thomas Aquinas, one of the most prolific writers of the Catholic Church and someone we expected to be an involved and encouraging voice in the miracle mix, actually prayed for an early death after he was struck by a mystical encounter with the Divine. He was so overcome by the sheer force of God's presence during a Mass he was celebrating in Naples that, in spite of having built a brilliant career as a writer and philosopher, he resolved never to write again: "My writing days are over; for such things have been revealed to me that all I have written and taught seems of but small account to me, wherefore I hope in my God that, even as the end has come to my teaching, so it may soon come in my life." Not only did Aquinas leave the last chapters of his magnum opus, *Summa Theologiae,* which he had worked on for years, unfinished— but, shortly thereafter, his prayers were answered: he died.

Some four hundred years later, the genius Blaise Pascal also left an intriguing legacy surrounding the power of firsthand miracle experience. Like Aquinas, Pascal experienced an encounter with the Divine in his own Night of Fire. Pascal thought belief in God was a personal choice, albeit one with probabilities attached. In what has come to be called "Pascal's Wager," Pascal, who was known as a bit of a gambler anyway, suggested that belief in God carried with it infinite gain, accompanied by only a finite amount of risk. He suggested that if you just risk a little by making yourself vulnerable and believing in God, you have everything to gain.

Regardless of my having lived in Las Vegas for five years and wondering whether Pascal's real motive wasn't some sixteenth-century version of cosmic card-counting, his theory struck me as a really safe bet. His approach to religious philosophy centered on his belief that truth is revealed not only by reason but also by the heart, and it is through this intuitive knowledge that we come to know God. Pascal's enduring contributions to science and mathematics—alongside his famous quote, "the heart has its reasons which the mind does not know"—seemed to reflect his understanding of both the spiritual and the material sides of the human equation.

This was the essence of the miracle debate that Katie, Meb, and I were having with each other. Through Pascal, Katie accepted that she didn't have to relinquish her affinity for the scientific method just because she saw the possibility of believing with her heart.

Meb, on the other hand, thought Pascal was so obvious that he bordered on being boring. After hearing his story, she immediately asked, "Why wouldn't you believe in something you experienced with your heart? Many of us call that 'love.'"

I was just happy to have finally found someone in my pile of Smart Guys who could begin to shed some light on my personal miracle struggle between faith and reality.

Pascal used his Night of Fire experience as the basis of a treatise on faith which he began but never completed, due to his unexpected death at age thirty-nine. All that remained of his experience with the

Divine was a piece of paper sewn into his jacket with the essence of his encounter. Meb and I were astounded when we realized that we, too, had had life-transforming experiences on the actual anniversary date of Pascal's Night of Fire with the birth of our first-born children—albeit three centuries later. Not only did we have a clearer understanding of how one event could change a life, but we connected with Pascal in a new way, and we both hoped he'd been able to collect on his now-famous wager.

Eerily, a "death by miracle" theme began to emerge. Not only were religious and scientific leaders affected, but the mere fact of expressing an opinion on miracles seemed to have been risky for anyone bold enough to venture one. Over the years, numerous authors who wrote about miracles found themselves victimized, tortured, or meeting an untimely death.

This "death by miracle" idea was keeping me up nights worrying about what it could mean for the three of us. I felt like we had already tempted fate with Katie's rescue and Elizabeth's and David's recoveries. The voice inside me cautioned "Leave well enough alone." But when I told Meb and Katie about my fears, they gave me a different perspective: they found all this seriousness funny—not only the Wise Guys, as we now affectionately called them, but my nervous reaction as well.

"It's a good thing we're not men," Meb joked at one of our miracle meetings, "because no one will be looking for us."

Not to be outdone, Katie chimed in "If God were going to strike me down, He would have done it a long time ago, but for much better reasons."

Though I was still nervous about tempting fate and what the future might hold for the three of us, I did what I usually do—I kept on going.

Maybe Meb's mythical meanderings into the spirit world and the esoteric factoids she loved sharing had gotten to me; and while I didn't know a lot about Greek mythology, I did wonder if we had unwittingly unearthed Pandora's box in our miracle exploration.

Meb had studied Greek mythology; so, at one meeting not long after I had brought up the Death by Miracle theme, I thought she could shed some light on the description of Pandora's box from Joseph Campbell . . . "the divine gift of the gods to a beautiful woman, filled with the seeds of all the troubles and blessings of existence, but also provided with the sustaining virtue, hope."

"Hope," I told them, "is the easy part." I focused on hope not only because it was an intrinsic part of my optimistic nature, but because the rest of Campbell's description reinforced my growing concern: "And by a like miracle, so will each whose work is the difficult, dangerous task of self-discovery and self-development be portered across the ocean of life."

Across the ocean . . . to where? I wondered. That was the problem: I had started to worry about where this miracle chase would take us. I hadn't known the path of self-discovery was going to be dangerous; I had only thought it would be interesting. And, certainly, none of us had bargained for a possible early death or public ridicule.

Meb tried to tie together Pandora's box, my fears, and her own thoughts about darkness and light and the gifts they bring by sharing some of the research and writing she had done for her dissertation, connecting ancient Greek mythology with contemporary tragedies.

"Think about it," she said. "We connect light with happiness and light with the soul, so we fear the absence of light."

From my perspective she was preaching to the choir. I hate the dark—I always see lions, and tigers, and bears, and God-knows-what-else in the shadows once my imagination gets going.

"The Underworld," Meb continued, "is ruled by Hades and his young bride, Persephone. Hades abducted Persephone from her life on earth with her mother, Demeter, and took her into the world of darkness against her will. As the result of early Greek negotiation with the Divine, Demeter was able to free Persephone for part of the year. Persephone returns to her mother bringing the spring, but she must go back to the Underworld each winter."

Katie and I glanced knowingly at each other, understanding that Meb viewed this story as a parallel to her own loss. I was hardly reassured.

Greek mythology aficionado (Meb) or not (that would be Katie), I thought Campbell had captured our journey perfectly. In addition to Campbell, I was also immersed in reading about puritanical England, where no doubt the task of self-discovery had been pretty dangerous. This was even before I realized that I would be moving to the town next to Salem, Massachusetts, home of the infamous witch trials. It's a good thing we hadn't been in Salem back then, because with religious conformity dictated by law, I have no doubt that the three of us would have been burned at the stake.

Burning witches aside, the seventeenth century transformed the world from the Dark Ages. In spite of the restrictive environment that existed, a new philosophical approach was emerging. Deism acknowledged the existence of God, but without any religion or other article of faith attached, and urged priests to abandon the use of mysteries, prophecies, and miracles. Founded by the British ambassador to France, Lord Herbert of Cherbury, Deists were in clear violation of the laws of the time.

One member, Thomas Woolston, was tried and condemned for blasphemy due to his book *The Discourse on the Miracles of Our Saviour, In View of the Present Contest Between Infidels and Apostates*, probably because he pronounced some fifteen Gospel miracles fraudulent. Later, Peter Annet, another Deist, wrote an assault on miracles in the *Free Enquirer* (no, not the *National Inquirer*), which earned him the charge of blasphemous libel. He was put in prison, pilloried, made to do hard labor, then placed under a bond of security for life. This was considered a "mitigated" sentence in light of his poverty, his old age, *and* the fact that they liked him.

I also credit Lord Herbert with initiating another trendy "fashion of the times"—the impossibly long investigatory book title. While Augustine was happy to write *City of God*, Aquinas his *Summa*

Theologiae, and Pascal *Pensees,* Lord Cherbury's book was titled *On Truth, As It Is Distinguished From the Revelation, From the Probable, the Possible and the False.* In her typical tongue-in-cheek manner, Katie came up with our own working book title: *Women Baby Boomers Postulate What Wise Dead Men Have to Say About Miracles and Live to Tell the Tale,* to help us feel a special bond with the historical characters we were discovering.

By this time, I wasn't the least bit surprised to learn that John Toland's book titled *Christianity Not Mysterious: Or, a Treatise Shewing, That There Is Nothing In The Gospel Contrary To Reason, Nor Above It: And That No Christian Doctrine Can Be Properly Called a Mystery,* was published in 1696 anonymously. While the book titles were getting longer, at least the authors were getting smarter about their own safety.

It almost seemed that the Age of Shakespeare increased the lengths to which Deists went to disprove miracles. Charles Blount's book *Miracle, No Violation of the Laws of Nature* actually characterized the miraculous element as a fungus. Not to be outdone in the search for a natural explanation for miracles, Karl Friedrich Bohrdt invented the "Brethren of the Third Degree," where he pronounced that, just like the stagehands in any great magic show, the apostles were the people who assisted Jesus with his magic tricks. Reverend Brewer "disproved" miracles by showing that they had occurred in pagan beliefs. He suggested that "a source of legendary myths was in the habit of adaptation . . . [and] a favorite amusement was to adapt some heathen tale and spiritualize it." While the image of a lot of folks in long gowns sitting around after dinner telling miracle stories is pretty cool to me, these guys would stop at nothing to prove their point: according to these thinkers, miracles could be caused by germs, imaginary friends, mutations of pagan beliefs . . . the list goes on.

It didn't take long before the lowly masses responded to the musings of their more literary contemporaries and experienced miracles of their own. One of our favorite stories occurred in the

St. Medard Cemetery in Paris where the Jansenist priest, the Abbé de Paris, was buried in 1727. The much-beloved Abbé was reportedly in the habit of granting miracles to those who came to his grave and asked for help. By 1731, hordes of people were flocking to the cemetery seeking intercessions. A year later, King Louis XIII closed the cemetery by royal decree. Maybe he didn't like the competition, or perhaps he was afraid of too many commoners gathering at the same time. In either case, it prompted the graffito "By order of the King, God is forbidden to perform miracles in this place." I can just imagine the author of this sentiment, sneaking into the cemetery in defiance of the King's order, willing to take a chance because she understood what the king refused to acknowledge: that where miracles are concerned, only God decides where, when, and how.

Fortunately, the Royal Society of London was formed a few years later—none too soon, in my opinion—and represented a novel (and rational) approach to the extraordinary, in which they postulated that the laws of science could be seen as the laws of God. When I first read this, my first thought was that this must have made almost everybody happy. I expected the saints to be part of miracle lore, and the Bible too; but in addition, I found King Charles II, his charter to the Royal Society of London for the Improvement of Natural Knowledge, and Sir Isaac Newton as their leader! Still, as a second child (and therefore a born compromiser), as well as a lifelong peacemaker and negotiator, I thought the Royal Society was a smart, diplomatic solution. Katie and Meb thought it actually sounded like a really fun seventeenth-century version of San Francisco's Bohemian Club—but we knew neither would admit women.

I have not found the Wise Guys, by today's standards at least, to have "pushed the envelope," though in their day they were quite remarkable. The writing of these learned men is fascinating, yet also stifling—full of the pomposity of their own self-worth, hiding the essence of their beliefs behind anonymity or posthumous publication. The environment the Wise Guys constructed for us was limiting, not limitless. In our world, Katie, Meb, and I believe that anything is possible, and the experience of the miraculous is not to be diminished, but instead is to be recognized, cherished, and shared. This is why we couldn't find the answer to the question of miracles solely in the treatises of long-dead philosophers, statesmen, or scientists.

Sharing our newfound knowledge gave us some great opportunities to make fun of each other. I was convinced that talking about the mysteries of the universe could end in our untimely deaths by supernatural means. Katie was off figuring out why God died back in the day. And Meb spent her off-hours picking up shocking details about saints and sinners. We were cutting to the chase of our inner selves without the usual prerequisites of time and common experience to smooth over our rough edges or mellow our anxiety. It was like writing the CliffsNotes on Friendship, though, thankfully we found it hard to be too intense for too long when talking about the concept of miracles as the result of a fungus.

It was a welcome relief to know that there were plenty of varied opinions on miracles—divergent views and theories were everywhere. Some, like the poet John Donne, viewed nature as the work of God's continued providence: "the ordinary things in Nature[,] would be greater miracles than the extraordinary . . . and only the daily doing takes off the admiration." The chasm that existed between the Deists, who claimed that nothing was miraculous, and Donne's sentiment, in which everything was miraculous, seemed bottomless.

The paradox I faced—I was empowered by tackling a question that had engaged minds for centuries, but frustrated by the realization that there is no proven answer—was a difficult balancing act. I had set out to find answers, but had only come up with more questions. The words of the twentieth-century academic Louis Monden offered a good perspective to the grave (no pun intended) discussions between the empiricists (who judged miracles by scientific standards), the skeptics (who were unconvinced of their existence), the Deists, and the rest. "Miracles," he said, "like grace in general do not destroy nature, but liberate, enable, and renew it."

In spite of the teasing from Meb and Katie about my obses-sion with dead wise men, I charged ahead, a bit like a bull in a china shop. My library books became my security blanket as I carried them around with me to our meetings. Meb joked: "Are you sure you're not meeting someone at the library, Joan? You sure are there a lot these days. . . ."

"Funny, Meb," I laughed. There was so much to learn—but, as I had suspected, the increasingly complex reality of my world took over. Over the past year, I had made the most difficult decisions of my life because of David's near-tragedy. The recent months were a blur arranging the myriad details that a cross-country move encom-passes, both in departing and arriving, buying and selling houses, and arranging schools for our three children. Through all this, I had been carefully doling out whatever time I could find to write and research the concept of miracle. In some ways this saved me, and the intellectual engagement of our miracle meetings provided me with renewed energy.

I knew there was more out there than the stifling attitudes of some of the Wise Guys. It was time, as Meb says, to go "outside the box." Tired of the library, of reading old books, of theorizing about what had happened so long ago, when Katie suggested a road trip to Marin County to check out a real live shaman and healer, I was more than ready to go. And trust me, for a girl from Boston, Marin County, California is a great place to seek out the unusual.

3

Footsteps in the Sand

Who is the third who walks always beside you?
When I count, there are only you and I together
But when I look ahead up the white road
There is always another one walking beside you.

—T. S. Eliot, the waste land

KATIE

I guess when you're researching a lot of dead wise men like Joan was doing, you can get caught in a real time warp. I looked forward to showing her the Marin County I know, not the "crazy Marin" my Boston-roots friend has in mind. It's true—Mill Valley, the town where I spent my childhood, was once Marin's answer to Haight-Ashbury in San Francisco and Berkeley across the Bay. Here, the Sixties was definitely a movement, not just a decade. All the hippies, flower power, and people making-love-not-war made for an interesting backdrop to a child growing up with the rigid rules and rulers of Catholic Christianity. Besides, I knew the rules, and I was a rule-follower. Memorize the answers to the Baltimore Catechism, pray for the unbaptized Pagan Babies, go to Mass, go to Confession, and try really hard not to do anything worth confessing. Oh, and stay away from the hippie lady on the corner selling brownies.

Life was pretty simple: if you follow the rules, you go to heaven. Of course, nobody's perfect. When I was in second grade, I committed a mortal sin. That's right—*mortal:* I ate meat on Good Friday. As I recall, I was really hungry and wanted a hamburger, and, thankfully, I was out with my grandmother, the one who didn't seem to care much about religion. In the confessional, Father Scandal (not his real name) was not amused. If I'd had any notions that the Mortal Sin category carried leniency for eight-year-olds who ate meat on the wrong day, I was mistaken. His tirade on the seriousness of my transgression and his lecture on eternal damnation made quite an impression. I'm sure he made me cry. Yet even at that tender age, some part of me recognized the absurdity in the situation.

I managed to get through the rest of grade school without so much as a hiccup in the confessional, and Mill Valley, like the rest of Marin County, made its way out of the sixties—and the hot-tubbing seventies, for that matter. Today, the town is charming, nestled at the base of Mt. Tamalpais (called "Mt. Tam"), the prettiest small mountain I've ever encountered.

Once I graduated from grade school, I went to an all-girls Catholic high school where I contemplated becoming a nun myself. And then one day, my sophomore-year homeroom teacher (a nun, of course) told us that French kissing was a mortal sin. Eternal damnation for French kissing? After having experienced that particular sin myself, I deemed it a waste of the priest's and my time to ever confess it, much less promise to never "sin" again. In a time span of one year, I went from contemplating the notion of devoting my entire life to God to realizing that a complete break with the Church was my only option. Taking the Catholic Church disposition of "all or nothing" seriously, I chose "nothing" by default. That is, until 1989, when a newspaper headline-*cum*-photo forced me to rethink the matter.

Being spared "Death by Bundy," as Meb likes to put it, has a permanent effect, like a dye that slowly seeps into your skin until you see yourself and the world you inhabit in a different hue. No matter how hard you try, it won't wash out. You can never go back to the way you were before. Don't get me wrong: I didn't have a tearful reunion with my Catholic soul on the altar of the nearest church; but at least I arrived back at the steps. After all, the implications of my experience are not all spiritual. The devastation wreaked by such a person suggests a world that is mortal, transient, and random. At the same time, I had to seriously consider the concept of divine intervention. I could no longer ignore the bellman's sudden arrival on the scene and the words he spoke directly to me. The newspaper article about Ted Bundy affected me as though it had been a personal telephone call from God: "You might want to rethink the whole complacency thing, for your own sake if not for Mine." It wasn't easy to reconcile my experience with my rational mindset. And with this consideration came a new set of problems: Why me? Why was I spared? Surely, there were more worthy candidates for salvation. What about the women Bundy savagely murdered? Where was God for them? My questions were a persistent presence in my life by the time I let ten more years go by and Joan, Meb, and I decided to embark on our miracle quest.

Our miracle meetings were an exhilarating luxury to me, a dusting-off of what had used to be my intellect. For a few hours every week we traded errands, laundry, and the endless needs of family and volunteer pursuits for a few hours of spiritual reverie. We met in Joan's living room, which felt like our very own office because we were rarely there otherwise—the back yard and family room were more practical for our non-miracle-related get-togethers. Besides, she had all the "stuff"—the flipchart, special colored pens, and the fanciest coffee maker—for our morning meetings.

We each got to "check in" with any cool information we had discovered; then a more formal brainstorming session began about miracle types and stories, miracle-book titles, or actual assignments. Joan seemed to have absorbed whole volumes by the time we were a month into our discussions, throwing in terms like "theophany" as she captured our ideas on the big white paper.

"What the heck is a theophany?" I asked her.

"An act by which God makes Himself present in time and space," she read from one of her white index cards.

Joan went on to tell us transfiguration stories about Krishna, who opened his mouth to his mother and revealed the whole universe; and about Muhammad and his night journey and ascension into heaven.

I was incredulous that any of these stories could be true and was surprised to learn that the Judeo-Christian tradition hadn't been the only one to espouse the idea of transfiguration.

"It wasn't just transfiguration," Meb added. "Stories about the multiplication of food and virgin births are common themes in most faiths."

"It's really about truth. Joanie, put Truth up on the board." Meb was leaning forward in her chair. "What is truth and who defines it?"

"Good Lord," I thought, "I'm in way over my head with these two!" Meb and Joan set the bar high from the beginning, and I needed to catch up. I found the perfect book to start, *A History of God* by Karen Armstrong—not for the faint of heart, but I hung on her every word.

We had been meeting almost weekly for months when one May morning, comfortable and cross-legged on the floor, surrounded by my books and papers, I announced I was going to see a Shaman and Healer who had an office in Marin County.

"You're going *where*?" Meb's arm froze halfway to her mouth with her coffee cup in hand.

"Did you say 'shaman'?" Joan wanted to know.

"Yes, Shaman and Healer," I responded matter-of-factly. "My friend Susan suggested it. She kinda reminds me of you, Meb."

"Thanks," Meb smiled, a little unsure. "Is that a compliment?"

"Well, she is someone who looks for answers wherever she can find them, sometimes in unconventional places. I think that's a good thing," I told her.

"Wow," Meb teased, "I didn't know you had it in you. When are you going?"

I was hoping the two of them would come with me. Meb said she'd love to go, if only to see me out of my element, but with her schedule, just making our meetings was all she could do, and I knew that. Fortunately, Joan seemed motivated to get away from the library and the pressures of packing up her family for the coming move, which were beginning to build. I was thrilled to have her for a day to myself, since her last day here seemed to be approaching at warp speed.

I know Meb thought this trip was way out of my realm, and she was right. What Meb didn't know is that I was used to holding my breath and jumping off into the deep end. My sister Mary always says "Go big or go home." In some ways it was a family motto, and it served me well in a family of seven. Get in the game, even if you fall on your face. Stand up and be counted. Take a chance. It cured me of a natural reserve, which was a change that became crucial later, when I took a place at the bankers' table dominated by men. Eric Vormanns, the Shaman and Healer, was an opportunity for me to "go big," be bold, and not play it safe.

Meb, Joan, and I knew instinctively, and now through our research, that the Catholic Church did not have the market cornered on miracles, and the Wise Guys were not the only voices. When the Protestants made the break with the Catholics, they willingly left the miracle tug-of-war behind. But those pesky miracles seemed to ignore religious quibbling, occurring not just in both Protestant and Catholic faiths, but in many varieties of religion and personal spirituality around the globe. When the Protestants eventually brought miracles back, they gave them a different name: General and Special Providences. This was all a comfort to me, because I had a hard time believing in miracles if it meant you had to be Catholic to get one.

I knew little of Eastern or tribal philosophy and religion. But Meb seemed to, and she believed there would be valuable information for us from these rich traditions where miracles were concerned. I read a book on Buddhism by Deepak Chopra a few years back, written in language a karma dummy like me could understand. The book prompted me to imagine a different world, an invisible one made up of the energy generated from thoughts, or from our connection with the universe. Unfortunately, I experienced limited success.

However, my superficial foray into Eastern thought did come in handy, because from the start of our miracle meetings, Meb was also an enigma to me. She talked about miracles unfolding: the ripple effect. I had no idea what she was talking about, although I had some vague notion that energy was involved. I thought miracles either happened or they didn't, end of story. From the beginning I wanted to at least define our terms so that we could work from the same rulebook. The problem was that Meb had no rules where miracles were concerned, which confused and frustrated me.

I made our appointment with Eric Vormanns at his office in Fairfax, tucked on the northwest side of Mt. Tam. On an unusually stormy June day, Joan and I drove across the Richmond Bridge that connects the East Bay to Central Marin. I could see Mt. Tam through the clouds off in the distance.

"Joan, did you know Mt. Tam was named for a Miwok Indian princess? Legend has it that her full body profile can be seen on the ridge of the mountain, her long hair cascading down the north side and her legs extending out to the south." I spoke like a native, though I had struggled all through childhood to see the Indian princess myself. Of course, this didn't trouble me too much, since I didn't generally believe in things I couldn't see.

"It's too cloudy," Joan said as she strained to see the top of the mountain.

"I kissed my first boy on that mountain," I continued, "and saw a rattlesnake up close and way too personal. Our first house in California was on Mt. Tam." I was happy to share these life tidbits with my friend.

I thought about how different the two sides of the Bay were from each other; how, every time I crossed into Marin, Mt. Tam stood like a guardian for the surrounding communities, lush and green from bottom to top all year round, hiding the secret of the Pacific Ocean unseen on its west side. There was a trail called the Steep Ravine that ran all the way to Stinson Beach; completing that hike had been a badge of honor when I was a kid. I hadn't lived there in almost twenty years, but it still felt like I was going home.

We pulled into a wooded parking lot and entered a nondescript building. I was relieved to find that Eric's office could have been any doctor's office, with its small waiting area and patient exam room, except possibly for the striking African art on the walls. More importantly, Eric himself was warm, welcoming, and dressed like any Western doctor might be (minus the stuffy lab coat). Eric began by telling us about his life. Ironically, he had been raised Catholic alongside his training to become a great Healer, a gift recognized by the tribal leaders at his birth in a tiny village in Ghana on the Gulf of Guinea in West Africa, where he'd spent the first seventeen years of his life.

As a young child, he'd used water as his healing tool, pouring it into a calabash and placing his hand over the vessel, sending energy into the water. He saw this energy as colors. Always aware of the energy generated from the spirit world, he described to us the ocean's edge, where, from a very young age, he met his spirit guides, whom he called his friends. They offered him comfort, and he knew they were an extension of "the one true God." Though he learned the basics in school, he found the traditional linear way of thinking difficult—perhaps, he suggested, because it interfered with his intuitive knowing. As I thought about Pascal and his understanding that knowledge comes from the heart, I felt like I was beginning to fill in the blanks on a vast spiritual canvas.

Eric's grandfather also had "the gift" and could read footsteps in the sand. This was his grandfather's way of first examining, then healing his fellow tribesmen. As a healer, Eric had to be connected to what, for him, was this other very real world. This connection, one that had been with him always, is how he recognized that he had the gift to heal, to tap into the energy of this other world and to see things others could not.

He was patient with our questions. "How would you define a miracle?" "Is God involved?" "Do you believe in miracles?" When asked in an interview if he believed in God, Carl Jung once responded: "I don't have to believe. I *know!*" Eric, too, did not need to believe. Knowing was part of his being, before he had conscious thought, stitched into the fabric of his soul. Miracles, so called, were simply known, too, as part of the reality that Eric took as given and I had to work so hard to grasp.

As we were about to leave, he asked if either of us would like a "reading." I admit that I didn't fully understand all he was trying to convey. And even though I had evolved enough to believe in his abilities, I didn't want him placing his hands over me and seeing something that he couldn't hide, something that I wouldn't want to know. "No. No, thanks," I said. Joan hesitated a second before she answered, reminding me later that it was important to find out not only what he did, but why and how.

"Okay," she told Eric with a sidelong glance at me.

Joan was willing to be the guinea pig, even though I could tell she didn't want to, having confided in me how much she hates going to doctors' offices. Joan allowed me the more comfortable position of observer while she submitted herself to the powers of god-knows-what, and I was beginning to appreciate what a good partnership we shared. I couldn't wait to commiserate about all that Eric had alluded to in our interview.

Eric directed Joan to lie on the examining table in the room. He held his hands above her, moving them along an invisible plane six inches away from her body, just as I had somehow pictured he would. After several minutes, he was done. Joan got up and we said our good-byes. His demeanor had changed somewhat, however. He was not as calm as he had been, and he put his arm on Joan's shoulder and reminded her that Western medicine was good, too. "Make sure you check in with your family doctor." ("Right," I thought. Joan's normal schedule is crazy, and with the move it was now even crazier. "No way was a doctor visit making it onto The Schedule.")

On the ride back home, Joan and I mulled over our interview. "That was so weird at the end," Joan commented. "He must have known I wasn't feeling particularly well today." We laughed, a little uncomfortably—maybe he was for real.

I did believe that Eric tapped into a spiritual plane that's lost to most of us who are mired in our three-dimensional world. After meeting Eric, I could picture another world, one where form wasn't a necessity. This helped me, finally, to consider the possibility of angels, not as the mythical winged creatures you could see, but rather these spirit guides Eric knew so well, their goodness and wisdom extending all the way back to the Divine. I finally understood the concept of eternal guardians and messengers who cross the barriers we create between our spiritual and material existence, extending us a lifeline back to earth, so that even at our most vulnerable, maybe our most afraid, we are not alone.

The meeting with Eric allowed me to add dimension to my own story, though I suffer from a chronic insecurity in relaying it to others. I struggle against seeing myself as stupid and naïve in those moments, feeling embarrassed, and I hesitate to commit to the uncomfortably spiritual details of my escape. No wonder I am relieved when I hear about another person saved like I was, pulled from the brink by some power we cannot possibly understand.

When I explained my miracle chase to another friend, she suggested I read *Expecting Adam* by Martha Beck. Full of the kind of spiritual awareness Eric had demonstrated, I was especially intrigued by an experience Ms. Beck relayed about her dramatic escape from a fire in her high-rise apartment building. Carrying her toddler, several months pregnant with her second child, she is about to succumb to the heavy smoke in the stairwell when a man grabs her from behind and helps her down the final floors. He stays right by her side until they are safely outside the building. The next day, the story of the fire appears on the front page of the newspaper; serendipitously, she is shown in the accompanying photo emerging from the smoky stairwell. Aside from her son in her arms, she is alone.

The more stories I hear, the less insecure I become. Jim, who isn't the miracle-chaser type at all, told me about an exhibit he had just seen that his company was sponsoring about Ernest Shackleton. The accompanying film, about the great early-twentieth-century explorer of the Antarctic, mentioned an odd experience Shackleton had on his expedition. "You should check it out for your book, Katie," he recommended. Considering the source—Jim thought miracles had to hit you over the head with a two-by-four—I knew this could be good.

During his attempt to be the first to cross the Antarctic continent, Shackleton and his crew became stranded when their ship *Endurance* was trapped in ice floes. In a desperate attempt to save the lives of his men, Shackleton and two companions made a perilous journey to South Georgia Island to find help at a whaling station. After thirty-six hours of trudging through the ice and bitter cold without rest, and thanks to some rare clear weather, they reached the station. In Ernest Shackleton's own words, "I had no doubt that Providence guided us" (he was clearly Protestant). "I know that during that long and racking march of thirty-six hours over the unnamed mountains and glaciers of South Georgia it seemed to me often that we were four, not three." His two companions confessed to the same curious presence. They returned to rescue the remaining crew; and though it took nearly two years, all twenty-seven men returned safely to England. Shackleton's experience was memorialized by T. S. Eliot in his epic poem *The Waste Land*:

> *Who is the third who walks always beside you?*
> *When I count, there are only you and I together*
> *But when I look ahead up the white road*
> *There is always another one walking beside you*

My visit to Eric was an epiphany of sorts—not as an isolated event, but rather as the culmination of my first months of miracle-chasing. Meb had forced me to think, really think, about what her view of miracles meant, and somehow my teensy exposure to Buddhist thought not only made more sense, but left me wanting more. Immersing myself, not unlike Joan; soaking up whatever I could find: Islam, Judaism, the mystics and their journeys to seventh heaven, and, of course, other credible "strange stories" offering me relief from my self-imposed miracle malaise. I was even starting to peek into a few science books to see if it were possible to believe in miracles and embrace all things scientific at the same time. My study of miracles was allowing me to see possibilities where before I could see only cold facts. I was gaining a bit of confidence about my own weird tale, and it felt good not to be alone. Putting it all together alongside the substantive miracle talks Joan, Meb, and I were having together, meeting Eric became my "Aha!" moment. You might say I was seeing footsteps in the sand, not clearly defined—but I knew they were leading somewhere worthwhile.

4

A MOTHER'S TRUST

Where there is great love, there are always miracles.

—WILLA CATHER

MEB

You know you have true-blue friends when they make fun of your thinking, poke at your heart, push your boundaries, and then turn right around and tell you that the way you see the world gives special meaning to their lives. I was touched by Katie's tentative foray back to Marin, and with a non-Western healer to boot. Significantly, this visit was Katie's idea, with Joan just going along for the ride. Personally, I tend to be put off by trendy New Age spiritualism, and I wondered if Eric might be another fringe spiritualist, preying on the rich and disaffected Marinites. On the other hand, I deeply respect tradition and ritual and appreciate native and folk spirituality. So I was intrigued by the possibility of this being the real deal. But since I was frying a plateful of fish in my life just then, I decided there was, unfortunately, no way I could go with them.

At our next meeting in Joan's living room, I was in a funk. I was thinking about Joan's move and wondering how it would change our miracle chase together.

"Eric," Joan said, interrupting my thoughts. "Such a simple name for such a complex person. He had a nice way about him, a feeling of peace."

"I thought it was a little spooky," said Katie.

"Katie can be such a wimp sometimes," Joan chuckled. "I've always hated medical exam rooms, and yet I was the one who had to volunteer to lie on the exam table and let Eric do his healing 'thing' over me." They laughed. "This part was spooky," she went on. "He had his hands out just over my body, like he was feeling some energy thing or something. I felt him pause; he seemed to stop as his hands hovered over my heart. He made me wonder if something was wrong."

When she said that, I wished I had gone too. If only my own heart could be healed by someone's hands. "Get over it," everyone said, but I could not put my finger on what *it* was. Maybe someone like Eric could tell me.

On the outside, I was a generous, intense, and demanding friend. Friendship, to me, was as much about loyalty and being there for one another as it was about fun. If someone didn't understand how my life with Liz, Andrew, and Daniel was further complicated by Bob's travel schedule, they did not get close to me. If someone didn't understand my quirky sense of humor, they did not *want* to get close to me.

When Joan took me in like a social worker and made me her personal case, life truly became more enjoyable. She has a wonderful capacity for connecting people over fun experiences. On the outside, I had it all together, had it all; what was the problem? But on the inside, I was so lonely. Not many people knew that I stayed up until almost midnight helping my obsessive daughter complete every last homework problem for the next day before she would go to bed, reading reams of printed material to her since so much she was required to learn was not available in Braille. Few knew how I worried about her brothers, how they often spent evenings alone in the other room, doing homework or watching TV, missing out on regular family time. Even fewer knew how hard I tried to make life as "normal" as possible. I found ways to adapt to everything and to accommodate everyone, from how to make sure Liz could match clothing colors, to how we all might participate in vacation activities, even finding special recipes for my mother-in-law's allergies for Thanksgiving dinner, decorated and cooked in a Martha Stewart style.

It was true that by now, finally, some of my efforts were paying off, because Liz was doing well in her new high school. She seemed happier than she had ever been, and I had hopes that she would make good friends. As Joan pointed out, Andrew and Daniel were growing up to be great people; good at sports, with good friends, and, even by suburban standards, getting good-to-great grades. I was starting to feel a sense of okay-ness that I had never felt before. Nothing to worry about; I told myself I could breathe for the first time in at least ten years.

Joan decided to go along with another one of my Martha Stewart fantasies, and we giggled our way through the preparation for David and Andrew's eighth-grade graduation by making chocolate-covered strawberries for the school party. After spending what seemed like hours making the hundred-and-something we had committed to, we only had seventy-five done.

"Joan," I whined, "I gotta go. This is enough. These kids don't need so many; I never even saw a chocolate-covered strawberry until my wedding day!"

"Oh, no, my friend," said Drill Sergeant Joan. "We said we would do a hundred, and we will." (I knew there was no way I'd ever committed to do a hundred—that goal would be Joan's.) I fully expected her to say "Now drop and give me twenty-five more."

You see how Joan became the Parents' Club favorite? She was the go-to gal that every school has and needs, that will fill in and finish what the less-committed commit to and don't quite complete. So I stayed, putting the extra effort into doing something for Andrew instead of Liz (and liked how that felt). When we got to ninety-something, Joanie's mom, who I secretly wanted to adopt, walked into the kitchen.

"By the way, there are some strawberries I moved into the dining room for the two of you to eat."

Sure enough, right there on the dining room table were twenty-five chocolate-covered strawberries Joan's mom had sneaked onto a tray to make sure we had some for ourselves. Always thinking, at least about Joan, this mom knew the balance of pleasure and work, a kind of self-care that Joan had learned but I had not: to work hard but have fun doing whatever it is that you do. And although Joan was living proof of working hard and having fun, I could see in the pace of her life what she had become in the process: the human personification of the Energizer Bunny, going and going and going. Joan thinks she can always do more—she just sleeps less.

I already knew how to be someone who keeps going and going. I had learned and become proficient at pushing myself. I began to realize, though, that Joan could show me how to work hard for myself—and she was a good enough friend that I was willing to let her. Both of us being "slightly" competitive, Joan found a personal trainer we could share (something I needed but Joan did not need). Now that we knew she was leaving for the East Coast, our training sessions became a way to spend time together combining work and play, her specialty, before she left me. I felt as though Gene and his new job in Boston were forcing my greatest friend to abandon me. I was furious at him for tearing her away; at the same time, I was terrified that I would, in the end, lose her completely.

In the meantime, we continued our commitment to our training program. Admittedly, getting me to the gym was harder for Joan than our actual workout. On one particular visit, I was surprised when she asked if I had seen any changes in the area of the ever-important pectoral muscles, because she had. While Joan was sore in a few key spots, I, on the other hand, felt pain every time we went to the gym—even before we got started. It figured that skinny Joan would see the first actual results.

Typical Joan, her days were packed full with much more than our time together as she readied to move again. She still had the fast-paced program of getting her kids to activities, volunteering at school, managing the nonprofit she had worked to save from extinction, and cooking up fun things to do with friends. Now she had added relocation to the list. For all three of us, miracle-chasing started to take a back seat to the end of the school year, as we felt ourselves having to chase around after kids and husbands who kept demanding more attention.

As he transitioned to Boston, Gene needed to attend an increasing number of professional events, including an anniversary celebration one evening for a venerable venture capital firm. The next day when we met for our miracle meeting, Joan made a connection back to Eric. She told us she had brought up the topic of miracles at the party and commented, "You know, venture capitalists (VC's) are a lot like bankers, Katie, but with more imagination." (We loved poking fun at Katie's bottom-line personality.) "These guys live up in the stratosphere with a master-of-the-universe approach to the world around them. At one end of the spectrum, there's Eric and his footsteps in the sand; and on the other end of the spectrum, there are the VC's who are so out there—they're even beyond Meb." Joan smiled as she nudged me.

"So, what did they think about miracles?" I asked, ignoring the ribbing. "I would think that to be a good venture capitalist, one would do well to be open to all possibilities."

"Oh, a few actually got into it," said Joan. "But to be fair, it isn't the type of topic one usually discusses at these events."

Struck by the contrast between the two worlds, the spiritualism of Eric and the temporal reality of the VC's, I reminded the two of them, "I think it was Thomas Moore who said 'Spiritual knowing is more a matter of unknowing, often requiring the sacrifice of our hard-won rational knowledge'."

On this, Eric and the venture capitalists would probably agree. Moving forward sometimes means we have to address old issues in new ways and try out things others say will never work. It takes being fearless about the possibility of failure, a willingness to face the unknown and add whatever is found there to the equation.

The juxtaposition of the otherworldly realm of Eric and the natural world of the VC's brought us back to the fundamental debate about miracles. Again and again, we asked ourselves: is a miracle a part of the fabric of life, or a constructed exception to the dictates of nature? No matter how much coffee we drank together, the answers to our rhetorical questions about what miracles are, and how they work, remained elusive: with every new discovery, we had even more questions. We were chasing a moving target.

I was happy that my friends were stepping outside their comfort zones to explore a new world of healing and miracles—auras, even, for heaven's sake. As delighted as I was, their enthusiasm for the intangible had the effect of making me feel more adrift, wanting to seek solid ground. I was growing tired of being expansive and limitless. Uncharacteristically, there were no words I could share; I felt bereft, as if the ground were shifting under my feet.

Loath to give the two of them one more eye-rolling opportunity at my expense, I didn't tell them about my attempt to find an answer to this ennui by opening the Bible and pointing to a passage for direction. I had learned about this type of communication with the Divine while reading a book on Augustine. It surprised all three of us when, suddenly, I announced that I wanted to learn more about this Doctor of the Church and his mother.

I can't really say what drew me in; it just seemed like an important next step for me to take. I knew that Augustine was a theologian and a philosopher. Katie had piqued my interest when she reported that where miracles were concerned, Augustine was "the authority to which later writers would always return." As I brought Augustine into the miracle mix, all three of us would develop a love/hate relationship with this man. Katie had a hard time getting beyond seeing Augustine as singlehandedly creating an environment of misogynistic, patriarchal elitism she saw as evident in the Church today. ("Don't let them fool you; it wasn't 'singlehanded,'" I tell Katie.)

Joan didn't appreciate his dogmatic reputation, but liked the fact that he was able to change his mind about miracles. ("A religious politician, if ever there was one," I tell Joan. "Reminds me of the popes in the Middle Ages.") Augustine wasn't perfect, but my intuition told me that he was going to teach me something noteworthy about my miracle.

I discovered that when he first started writing about miracles, Augustine believed that they no longer existed in the world. He felt that in the time of Christ and the Apostles, miracles were performed to show Christ's divinity; once this was established, they were not needed any more, and so they did not occur. Then later, toward the end of his life, Augustine wrote that "miracles are so numerous even in these times that we cannot know about all of them or enumerate those we know." This is more like what I believe. Better late than never, I always say. I was determined to learn what caused this dramatic shift in his thinking because most men I know find it hard to admit that they've made a mistake. I told Joan and Katie that I bet Augustine had a personal miracle experience or two up his sleeve. He was heady and intellectual, looking for proof—then, poof! I was determined to find out what had happened.

Augustine is a fascinating psychological example of a person who decides to walk "the road less traveled," only to find out that many others are right there on the road along with him. The language is different; but reading the account of his life after he left home, I cannot help but think of a certain group of idealistic young men I knew in the sixties and seventies, entering the world of the American Freshman Far Away from Home. It is a time of change; there are cultural forces that pull you along with them. And your rationale for trying new things becomes "Everybody's doing it."

Here's how Augustine puts it: "I went to Carthage, where I found myself in the midst of a hissing cauldron of lasciviousness. I ran wild with lust, the abominable things I did: rank depravity, a surfeit of hell's pleasure. Bodily desire like a bubbling swamp and virile sex welling up within me."

An active, ahem, mind should not have to be accounted for; but then, as now, it is not always appreciated—seriously, brilliance can be a burden for the person who is truly gifted, as Augustine seems to have found. But by his own admission, Augustine is also lazy, living in the present moment. His intellect urges him to seek the Truth, and some of his questions are answered by Plotinus and the Neo-Platonists; these folks see goodness and reality as transcendent, with the One as the highest reality. It is heady stuff, but not completely fulfilling.

With encouragement, no doubt, from his Christian mother, Monica (or maybe he just wants to get her off his back), Augustine begins to read the Epistles of St. Paul and finds some answers there. While Augustine is seeking truth and pleasure, Monica has been praying nonstop for him to convert to Christianity. Augustine truly loves his mistress and son, but he thinks there is something to all this Christian stuff. Beyond this dilemma, who would not be conflict-ridden when they have "lustful and lascivious" feelings, a mother like Monica, and an alcoholic and noteworthy womanizer for a father? The tension between how he lives and the answers he seeks becomes unbearable; he nearly has a nervous breakdown.

God saves him with a miracle. At the point of tearing his hair out, Augustine gets the "Call." He is in a secluded garden when he hears a child's sing-song voice.

"*Tolle, legge. Tolle, legge,*" he hears. "Take and read it. Take and read it."

What is it? Suddenly Augustine understands. He opens a Bible and turns to a page. He knows that the lines he first reads are for him and him alone.

It says: "Not in rioting and drunkenness, not in lust and lewdness, not in strife and envy. . . . Instead, take unto you the Lord Jesus Christ, and spend no more time thinking of the flesh in order to fulfill its lust."

With Love, St. Paul (last part, mine).

It seems that a miracle can be a powerful equalizer. Just like Katie and her newspaper article, the thunderbolt miracle appears. Take and read. Take and read. And wake up.

History tells us that Augustine immediately converts to Christianity, but I personally doubt it. After all, he admits to loving his common-law wife and son. I don't think he just converts and dumps them both on the spot. He's a saint, but he is also a man of his own season and time. When he finally commits to his new celibate life, he turns his considerable intellect and obvious passion toward writing numerous volumes, in detail, on all things religious, from a Christian point of view. Later, the Church would reward him with the title Doctor of the Church for his profound impact on Catholic doctrine. Not only could Monica say that her son finally converted, but then she could add "My son, the doctor. . . ."

It seems to me that Monica is the epitome of a persevering mother. When her married life is less than fulfilling, she focuses her attention on her three children and on developing her spiritual life. Unlike moi, Monica was well respected in her community for maintaining a sweet disposition in spite of her circumstances. I think Monica found a way to be her own person, and this now makes her far more interesting to me than Augustine.

With my own three children "launching" soon, I find myself thinking more and more about this woman who doggedly follows her adult son from dock to dock, port to port, city to city, trying to convert him. Any mother who has had the experience of getting her wayward son to agree to come to a Thanksgiving dinner, only to find out that he has ditched the "fam" for the girl, can resonate with Monica. In fact, she was such a devoted mother that the Catholics rewarded her with sainthood too. (Did I mention that Joan, Katie, and I attend Saint Monica's Church?)

I can see Monica now on *Dr. Phil:*

"Why do you follow your adult son around North Africa, forcing him to board boats that set sail in the wee hours of the morning just to escape you?"

"Convert, Augustine, convert," she says, ignoring Dr. Phil.

Augustine responds, rolling his eyes as only sons can, "Okay. Okay. 'God, give me chastity, but not yet'."

Mothers reportedly have a tendency to make their children into saints, at least in their own minds. But at least to my mind, having a son actually become a saint makes Monica something else (though she is definitely still over the top). I think of her as a kind of Wonder Woman of her time because she never gives up on the person she knows in her heart her son to be. I am sure some part of her life is sacrificed as she spends years filled with worry and prayer. Christ said "She who loses her own life shall gain it." We all have ideas of what our lives will be like: then we get married and have children. I don't think we ever know what life will really ask of us. Only faith helps us respond to our challenges in a way that makes the world better, not less so. At this point in our miracle journey, knowing about Monica helps me go on, seeing that the life I imagined and feel I have lost may not be the life I am called to live.

As I chase miracles, I find solace in reading about all sorts of religious women, Christian, Sufi, Hindu—Monica types. No matter how obsessed or unusual they may seem to be, I recognize a familiar face in their ability to hold fast to dreams. For me, Monica becomes emblematic of the knowledge that, with enough hope, faith, and prayer, I can sustain a vision of who I really know I am, of who I believe my loved ones to be, of my children finding their way. With enough faith, things will right themselves in the end. The risk I take of being Monica-like—that other people might think I am too intense, or too obsessive, or outright nuts for being so committed—outweighs the darkness that would ensue if I did not give this life my all. As Willa Cather says, "Where there is great love, there are always miracles." We are asked in this life to give Great Love.

For me, the unfolding miracle of Elizabeth weighs heavily on the choices I now make. She is my Augustine, filled with promise, and I am her Monica, not willing to let her abilities languish. Who I am as a woman is caught up in the day-to-day of being a wife, and being the mother of three wonderfully gifted, active children, and the added demands that come with raising a child with a disability. The woman I believed I was when I first got married has been channeled into taking what has happened in our family and making sure it will not happen to another family: to live on, in the best way, no matter what. To not let the "bad guys" win.

It is true that my mother (and apparently John Wesley) always said "Work like everything depends on you, and pray like everything depends on God." I have come to interpret this as meaning that I should work to follow my life's path and pray for God to show me this path every day.

Sometimes the path is not obvious. If someone had asked me in 1983 if I thought I would become a child advocate, I would have said that I planned a career in higher education. Distraught by the cavalier sentencing of the abusive nanny and the judge's unwillingness to restrict her from future contact with children, I became politicized and responded in the best way I could to what I believed to be an outrage against humanity.

When Liz was shaken by our neighbor's nanny, there was no way for a child's parent to legally know if they were hiring the same person who abused—no, tried to murder—my daughter. This was an impossible situation for me. When the judge told the nanny to be a nanny again, I experienced a sudden sickness and a sudden knowing at the same time: it was wrong, and I would stop it. There needed to be a way for parents to know that they might be hiring the person who tried to murder a baby: my baby.

I see now that this was my Call; this, too, was part of our miracle. Listening to the judge in the courtroom say that it wasn't like my baby had been sighted for very long, so she would not now really miss her sight, was an alarm that called me to wake up and start a journey that would take me far beyond anything I could have imagined for myself.

On a path that twisted and turned, full of characters and courageous volunteers, that Call started a process that eventually resulted in a statewide program in California called Trustline (www.trustline.org). The California Trustline Registry is a way for parents to check to see whether the person they wish to hire to care for their child has a criminal or child-abuse history. The statistics speak for themselves when it comes to the program's impact: hundreds of children have been spared from child abusers, rapists, sexual offenders, even convicted murderers. I learned that if I could just take one step and then another, trusting that I was the instrument for a change that needed to happen, I could achieve what some thought impossible. The idea that three state departments could collaborate and implement a program together and that two legislators, as far right and left as they come, would passionately co-author legislation, was seen as a stunning victory to some and as an act of God by others. Since this legislation (fifteen bills in all, and still counting) was never about me, I was never afraid.

In spite of my anger, grief, and oh-so-many sleepless nights, there were countless miracles along the way that propelled me forward. Take the afternoon just before a very important hearing in Sacramento: We had been lobbying for two weeks, calling every member on the committee. As it stood, the Democrats did not want the legislation because it "impinged on the rights of felons" by conducting background checks on potential caregivers, and the Republicans did not want the bill because it "would cost too much." We had made inroads among the Northern Californian legislators who had already heard from hundreds of parents, but we had less of an impact in Southern California and needed help. I had made contact with a prominent doctor in San Diego who specialized in child abuse. He had given me some names to generate support, but I had not found the time to call any of them. It was so hard to say "Hello, this is Mary Beth Phillips; my daughter was abused by a neighbor's nanny and I am working on trying to prevent this from happening to someone else." Just thinking about it made me cry.

I never watched television in the daytime back then, and still don't; but this day, perhaps out of my loneliness and anxiety, I needed a distraction. I was nursing my son Andrew in the family room, feeling warmed by the sun coming in through the west windows. Liz was riding her galloping Clip Clop the Wonder Horse, enjoying the rhythm of the back-and-forth movement and the auditory clop sounds it magically made, along with an occasional whinny. My attention was suddenly drawn to the documentary on the TV. There was a young mother with a son who also had been shaken by a caregiver. Listening to her story, I soon realized that this was Cheri, one of the very women the doctor had suggested I contact! The miracle might have been that I caught this bit of television, but even more miraculous was that I could locate where I had written her number on the back of something in the piles of paper on the kitchen desk.

We were moving the next week so that Liz could attend a pre-school for children with visual impairments, and everything was boxed up. Undaunted, Cheri came up for the hearing and stayed overnight with us. I remember her telling me her traumatic story. It was so upsetting and so like my own that my immediate visceral reaction was to be violently sick in front of her. Not the ideal first impression.

Never remotely involved in politics before, I was just following my heart. I had called and called the office of the committee chair, Tom Bates, convinced that if I could just speak with him, he would understand and support us. First, he was out of the office. Then he was not available. No one would even speak to me. I was something of an oddity, a woman who had the audacity to think that she, a common citizen, could change the way the State of California did business.

The day before the hearing, I was up early, trying to keep things normal, even though I was so agitated that I was crawling out of my skin. I thought I would follow up with a call to the press person who might send a camera crew to film our trip to Sacramento, since they might be interested in covering "the unusual grassroots effort" these crazy mothers were doing. I had little Andrew on my hip as I dialed the number and waited while the phone rang.

"Tom Bates's office."

Tom Bates? He's the chair of the committee we are going to testify before and the guy I could never manage to talk to! I recalled how his staff person had told me that this legislation "will ruin the underground economy of the State of California." But here I had his office on the phone at 7:30 in the morning. I knew I had been trying to call the press contact, not the office of the committee chair. A miracle. I tell myself: this is clearly meant to be.

Like a coach, I focus my efforts. Give it all you've got, girl.

"Hello, there," I respond. "My name is Mary Beth Phillips. Could I speak with Assemblyman Bates, please?"

"Speaking."

The next day, my family, Cheri, and I drove to Sacramento early. We marched into offices of committee members and found staffers with pictures of children on their desks. We pleaded with them to ask their bosses for their vote. At the hearing, the vote was unanimous: the bill had passed its first major hurdle and was on its way to becoming law. It is a wonderful example of riding the wave, of allowing the unfolding of a miracle to work through you. It was the first time I realized that a coincidence could be a miracle in disguise.

Ten-plus years later, I look back and know the hand of God. For me, the Miracle Lesson seems really simple: it is about taking the next step and trusting in the unfolding of the Miracle itself. It is being like Monica, absolutely *all in,* heart, mind, and body; being patient and focused, knowing you are on a path that is meant to be and one you are called to take. It's trusting that even though things can be rough, God has a plan. Unlike other areas in my life, where even I can see that I try to control outcomes, in this one path—to make the protection of children a reality—I learn to be more trusting because I am sure I am not alone. Like Katie's hero, Shackleton, I feel Someone is always walking by my side.

One day, as I was cleaning the kids' bathroom, I received a phone call. "Mrs. Phillips?" the voice said. "Yes," I replied. "We want to honor you at the White House for the work you have done on behalf of women and children."

That's how I see my life, from "cleaning the house" to "being honored at the White House" in one easy "Call."

While I knew that Katie admitted the presence of a miracle in my life, she had a hard time figuring out just what it was. I think she thought that all that was happening to my family and all that I had accomplished was somehow not miraculous—it had been just the product of my hard work and perseverance. While I appreciated her confidence in me, I knew better. Joan struggled with the idea that God would bother interfering in our world at all, that divine intervention could reach into the ordinary. She didn't think that miracles came in the form of someone calling me at just the right moment, or finding an advocate for Trustline by just happening to watch a TV show at the right time. Joan wanted to believe in miracles, but she didn't have a worldview that included seemingly random events as miraculous ones. Not yet.

As Cardinal Newman says, ". . . it is incomparably more difficult to believe the Divine Being should do one miracle and no more, than that he would do a thousand." I suspect that Augustine changed his mind because he saw real miracles, many of which came to his attention because of his role as bishop. To me, Augustine should be a Doctor of the Church precisely because he had the integrity to change his mind and speak out.

Still, it's difficult to understand God's miracle nature in the modern world. That God should do more miracles for me seems more than I deserve. I do ask, though. I am world-weary and recognize that I really want a happy, "normal" family in the worst kind of way. I realize that my family is faltering under the weight of something, but I can't quite put my finger on it. Trustline is firmly established and the kids are all in good places, but I still feel anxious. Chasing after miracles has opened the awareness that I might need some kind of miracle for myself.

"Monica," I pray, "what can I do?"

My friends thought a weekend away would be good for me. Alas, it did not look like it would be all three of us going, because Joan's moving date was right around the corner.

For a goodbye gift to my friend, I gave her a plate inscribed with a traditional Irish blessing: "May the road rise up to meet you, may the wind always be at your back, may the sun shine warm upon your face, and rains fall soft upon your fields. And until we meet again, may God hold you in the palm of His hand."

It seemed fitting, coming from a Celtic girl who in fifth grade changed her name, for no apparent reason, to Meb. (Apparently, this poor girl could not spell, for the great Irish queen, a legend, is named Medb.)

After Joan's move, I seemed to need more time in my garden. Here, Liz and I had created a "tactile experience," where every plant or tree makes a sound, has an interesting and wonderful texture, or has a unique aroma. It's here, amid the beautiful colors, where I feel close to God—where I pray the best.

Finally, after weeks of planning, Katie and I headed off to Carmel for the weekend to read and to write. On a walk, through the charming streets and by the sweet-smelling ocean, Katie told me how fearful she was that her wonderful life might be taken from her at any moment. She lived with a sense of doom, irrational and real. I was really surprised; it had never crossed my mind that she carried this kind of fear within her. Not quite coming clean about my own fear and uncertainty, I shared with her some new thoughts I had about the dark night of the soul that John of the Cross writes about—how, even for saints, fear and loneliness can take the joy out of the miracles we have been given.

By now, each of us, in our own way, has begun to appreciate the reality that in order to better come to grips with chasing miracles, we first have to come to grips with ourselves. It's a part of the journey we have not expected.

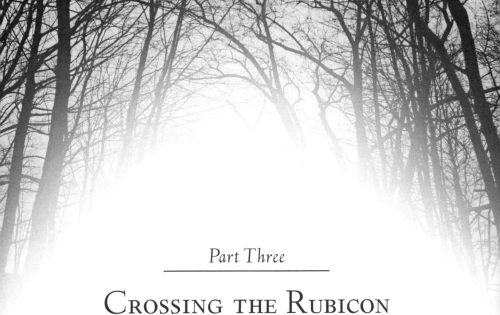

Part Three

CROSSING THE RUBICON

So it is a sort of Rubicon. One goes across; or not.
But if one does, there is no manner of security
against miracles.
One may be in for *anything*.

—C. S. LEWIS, MIRACLES

5

THE WIDOW MAKER

Who knows but life be that which men call death,
And death what men call life.

—EURIPEDES

KATIE

At our last meeting before Joan left, she told a parable about a widow who asked Buddha to raise her son from the dead. He agreed—if she could come up with a mustard seed from any family in the surrounding villages who had not experienced the death of someone close. The widow was discouraged when she could not find a single family in the first village that had not lost someone they loved. As she went door to door throughout the second village, she found the same response, and she began to feel a kinship with all those she encountered. By the time she had searched the third village without being given a single mustard seed, she realized that she didn't need her son to be brought back from the dead after all.

"Somehow, suffering is shared by everyone," Joan concluded.

"I think this beautiful story is about learning compassion," Meb suggested.

The three of us had talked about back-to-life miracles before. Meb really liked the idea, but every time she brought it up, I battled her. Stories about raising people from the dead were just too out there for me—we'd lose credibility, I said—but I also recognized some barrier in myself I couldn't get beyond, a hardness I didn't like. I think the parable was Joan's way of helping me soften that edge and open up enough to look at miracles in a different way.

When I went to the Hills' house the day before they left, the moving van loomed large in the driveway. I found Joan in her garage, amid the chaos of children playing hide-and-seek among the packing boxes, talking to one of the movers. "I just wanted to say an official good-bye," I announced, my words sounding trite and not at all like how I felt. I gave her a hug as the mover stood by awkwardly; I mumbled something about how busy I knew she was. I turned to go with a backward wave and quickly made my way back to my car just as the tears welled up.

Saying good-bye to Joan meant Meb and I were alone, without the maestro who had brought us together, the facilitator who conducted most of our meetings; they would now continue from Meb's house or mine with Joan on the phone, no flipchart or colored pens. I worried we wouldn't be able to generate the same energy the three of us created so easily when we were all together. I also knew I would miss my friend.

I've always looked over my shoulder when things seemed too good to be true. On the eve of my wedding, I had that feeling, like I somehow didn't deserve to be this happy. When my second pregnancy looked like it was going to thrive after the first had been marked by miscarriage and serious complications, I had the same feeling again. And then as Jim and I planned a trip to Italy with our best friends to celebrate our September anniversaries, I couldn't imagine that we would actually manage to go. Is that what survival guilt does to you? Kenneth Woodward, the author and *Newsweek* reporter, said that "to believe in miracles, one must be able to accept gifts freely bestowed and altogether unmerited." This is the only way I could believe that a miracle had happened to me and not have it conflict with my newfound faith.

We had begun to look at miracles from a historical perspective, but this was a way of keeping the subject impersonal for us. Meb knew better. She said that everyone has a "dark night of the soul." While it was not difficult to uncover mine, I didn't realize that for me to go forward with my faith, first I had to go back to the event that got in the way of my being able to make this whole miracle thing simple: a life experience that slapped me so hard and so completely that I was not the same person afterward. The struggles, contributions, and questions that I brought to our discussion could not be separated from it, and it was nearly impossible for me to have faith in the right way when I felt myself faced with a crisis in the present.

My father was fifty-four years old when he was diagnosed with terminal cancer. He died six weeks later. My dad would never know me as a fully entrenched adult, business successes and all, and he would never know me as the person I would become as a result of his dying. He would never know of my children. It's not that I didn't know that terrible things happen in this world. You cannot hear about the horrors of the Holocaust, or read the latest violent crime on the front page of the newspaper, without some feeling that our earthly existence comes with the worst of the worst. Still, the personal kick in the stomach my father's death represented to me provided a completely different level of understanding.

Although his death was bad enough, it was the dying itself that haunted me. When my father slipped into a coma, the doctors said he could last for days, maybe even weeks. So I was completely unprepared when I was summoned from work the very next day because his breathing had changed; his death could be imminent. I left work reluctantly, irrationally thinking that if I didn't go, he wouldn't die—that somehow I could make time stop.

Jim and I met at a parking garage in downtown San Francisco to drive the twenty miles to my parents' home in Marin County. I'm sure we must have spoken to each other, but all I remember is silence as I stared out the car window. Even the beauty of the Golden Gate Bridge could not help me focus on the present. When we arrived at my parents' home, the yard did not possess the usual promise of the season; once inside, the house seemed cold and unusually quiet, a harsh contrast to the scene we found upstairs. My father's room, where my brother, my mother, and a friend of my father's had assembled, was a waking nightmare, surreal and horrible. My father's eyes were open and rolled back, and his breathing was not labored, but gasping, like someone who had almost drowned and had just come to the surface for their first breath—only every breath was this way, a constant rhythmic barrage of violent gasps. I had to leave. I wanted to run fast and far, but only managed to make it to the back yard: to my father's own escape, his garden. Here, too, the garden looked stale and ready for the tending that should already have occurred in late March. Was it only a year ago that I had celebrated my wedding here? I wished I'd helped him weed more. He frequently asked me, but I always had an excuse. I sat in the nearest chair and stared down at the concrete patio. Yet again, I felt a compulsion to leave, to run away, as if this would somehow change the circumstances.

Jim joined me and interrupted my thoughts. "You know, if your father dies and you're not there, will you regret it?" he asked. I reluctantly made my way back to the room where my father lay dying in such an inexplicable way, my decision to return the lone rational force in the mess of irrationality that had overcome me. We all sat in the room with him. We waited. We couldn't help but hear.

Hours passed. Then, for no obvious reason—the noise of my father's breathing had not slowed or changed in any way—my mother, who had been holding his hand, bent over him and prayed the traditional Catholic blessing for the dead: "May your soul and the souls of all the faithful departed through the mercy of God rest in peace." As she spoke, my father's hazel eyes came down and rested on her with recognition and peace. I braced myself for another breath, but it never came.

For months afterward, I could not remember my father when he had been healthy. In six weeks, my memory of more than twenty-five years had been erased. I began to have a recurring nightmare. Each time, I was running down a dark and unfamiliar road, and I was being chased. I would finally find a telephone booth, scramble in, and dial my parents' home, only I could never get through—either the connection was lost or I would get a recording: "I'm sorry, the

number cannot be completed as dialed or is no longer in service."
And then I was out of time; whatever was chasing me was closer. I
felt more desperate and kept running. I always managed to find my
parents' home in these dreams. It was different—darker and mostly
unfamiliar—but I knew where I was and, briefly, I felt safe. Then I
would make my way up the stairs, open the bedroom door, and find
my father dying and making the terrible noise. It jolted me awake,
my heart pounding. His last hours of life had been singed into my
memory by the sound, this cacophony, an echoing boom that would
not leave me alone.

Some would say I was my father's favorite. We understood each
other in a way that transcended direct experience. We found the
same things to be funny, jokes that anyone would laugh at, but silly
mundane things too; and while my siblings found him to be unap-
proachable at times, I would barrel on through his irascibility to find
his soft side. I wasn't overly sensitive and I think this suited our relationship well. Whenever I walked into a room and he was there, I
felt a sense of belonging that was part unconditional love and part
knowledge of who I was at the core. After he died, I never felt that
connection again. I was no longer in a position to tread water, spiritually or otherwise. No one was going to pull me out or make me
swim or even save me from drowning.

The last time I had the dream, it started out the same way. I
was desperate and running from something terrifying and unseen.
But all of a sudden, the road became a familiar one, a frontage road
along Highway 101 in northern Marin County, and the dark was
lifting as I became aware that it was early morning. My fear subsided as the familiarity of my surroundings provided some comfort.
I was running to the cemetery where my father was buried. When
I reached the location of his grave, my father appeared by my side,
healthy again. He wore a gray suit, a white shirt, and his favorite red
patterned tie; I noticed his pressed white handkerchief in his suit's
breast pocket. He cleared his throat in his own particular way as he
put his arm around me and said "I'm so sorry, Kate. I love you very

much." His voice was so real that it too jarred me awake, but this time it was sweet cacophony.

I changed in meaningful ways because my father died when he did. I grew a heart. Maybe some people are born with true empathy, but I would not have counted myself among them. All of a sudden, I understood—not just intellectually, not with a grasp at sympathy, but I *understood* hardcore grief: "the dark night of the soul." Without my father around to give me that fix of belonging, I went in search of my soul, and not necessarily in some religious sense.

Although I wasn't so sure for many years, the answer to my husband's question in the garden that day is "yes"—I would have regretted not being there at my father's death. I feel blessed for the gift of seeing what happened in the end, all the ugliness of dying wiped away in that prayer and the memory of his final moment with us and, I believe, his first moment with God.

So, what does this have to do with miracles? When you come right down to it, miracles don't happen in a vacuum: they happen while we're living our lives, day to day. We really can't separate them from our messy, or tragic, or mundane, or happy lives, because this is where we search for meaning and *why* we search for meaning. All of us in the room when my father took his last breath saw what happened, and we each took something very personal away with us. I never forgot exactly what happened at the moment my father left us, even though I didn't know quite what to do with the experience at the time.

By the time our miracle-chasing was in full swing, I thought I had put my experience with my father behind me. Jim and I were planning a dream trip to Italy. We had never been to Europe together, and we had never left our children for as much as a week, much less two. I was in fantasy overdrive. Every romantic movie I could remember got rolled into one continuous video playing in my mind. There we were, running on some exotic beach, clinking champagne glasses on a terrace overlooking Lake Como, hiking up the olive-treed and Mediterranean-viewed Cinque Terra. *From Here to Eternity* meets *The Sound of Music.*

With less than a week to departure, Jim experienced some alarming symptoms during a run. His arms felt heavy, his chest felt "funny." The symptoms subsided, and he decided to check it out later, after his East Coast business trip that week. Finally, two days before we were leaving on our Italian adventure, he checked in with our family doctor, who performed a routine EKG. In non-medical terms, he flunked it. The following morning, a stress test revealed a serious blockage, and nitroglycerin was required to stabilize his heart. We would need to wait two long days before an emergency angiogram could be scheduled to see the extent of the problem and determine whether or not it could be fixed without open-heart surgery.

With all this "faith talk" and our recent experience with Joan and her son, you might think that life could throw me a curve and I would respond with loyalty and trust in God. If Joan hadn't moved to Boston by that time, maybe she could have helped me face-to-face. What does faith do for you in a crisis? How do you have faith that God will answer your prayers? If faith requires that you relinquish control—which is an illusion anyway—and accept the outcome as God's will, why pray at all?

I wish I could tell you that my faith saved me in this first real test. That I prayed earnestly and placed our lives in God's hands, "thy will be done" and all that. Instead, I was overcome with doubt. Looking over my shoulder when something seemed too good to be true revealed a monster in the making, not a trip to Italy. Evidently, arriving at faith is one thing—and exercising it is quite another.

I don't remember if I prayed at all on that Friday afternoon when my father died. If I did, I think my prayer would have been rejected for treason. At the time, I didn't think it had a chance of being heard, much less of helping in any way. I do remember feeling hopeless, a fatalist to either the whims of nature or the whims of God, whichever might be at work that afternoon. And while believing in

God and miracles has been a first step to lift myself out of spiritual limbo, prayer is quite another matter for me, complicated and murky: a foreign art form. This must be symptomatic of a childhood spent mired in memorized prayers. Mother Teresa said "If you have learned how to pray, then I am not afraid for you." Somehow the subtlety between memorizing and learning had been lost on me, not to mention the possibility of making up my own prayers to God, developing my own relationship.

Sometime after 1989, I started to talk to God, one-on-One. I admit this felt weird to me, intimidating and possibly irreverent. I gained new understanding for the prayers I had learned as a child. On good days, I can focus, I can petition for help for others, I can be thankful and really mean it. I can appreciate the beauty of the language in prayers like the "Our Father" or "The Prayer of St. Francis" and strive to mean those prayers too. I can also get stuck where praying becomes complacent or repetitive or obligatory. I often find myself starting a prayer—say, the Our Father—"thy kingdom come. . ." and the next thing I know I'm trying to figure out a way to remind myself to write down an appointment, only I'm drifting off to sleep and can't do it right away. So I start the prayer over because it doesn't seem quite right to start it in the middle—"on earth as it is in heaven"—and I realize I'm wondering if I left the oven on, or forgot to put the laundry into the dryer, or am thinking about the menu for tomorrow night's dinner. And then I start all over again. I don't usually do this at church because we say prayers out loud together, but I do get to the end sometimes and realize that I wasn't at all focused on what I was saying, even though I got through it from start to finish.

I may be prayer-phobic. I would say that I definitely have a confidence problem. I think there are holy people out there who are really good at praying, focused in a tenacious dog-won't-drop-the-bone kind of way, and if I were God that's who I would listen to: the holy, squeaky-wheel people. Why listen to the peons when you have people like Mother Teresa walking around? (Okay, I know, she's not walking around any more; but she can point to all the living saints that are.) And this is how I feel when life is good.

So, what happens when life is not so good? I am certain that for God's VIPs, there is not much difference between good times and bad, at least not in terms of how well they pray. Me? I found that I can go from laissez-faire and noncommittal to begging in a matter of minutes. Feeling really afraid has a way of sharpening prayer focus, quickly. This must be annoying to God, who must wonder why people like me can't focus like this all of the time. "I'm planning to work on that if and when this personal emergency passes. Did you hear that, God? I promise to get better at praying for other people, even random strangers who speak different languages. Meanwhile, if you could just give me a break here?" When you aren't practiced at praying, you evidently resort to bargaining and begging.

I knew enough to call in the reserves—Joan and Meb—when I realized I couldn't handle it on my own. I believe Joan is a VIP prayer. First of all, she has a good steady relationship with the Almighty, no fickle past there. She's on a first-name basis with Mary and half the saints, mostly the Italian ones, plus Bernadette. That's one of the great things about prayer. Even though Joan moved to Boston a month ago, she can do as much good from there as from here. Meb must say amazing and successful prayers in her garden, because it always looks like it is being tended by heavenly beings. Before Jim's operation, she brings us some of her flowers plus the Lourdes water that was sprinkled on David before his surgery. It's good to know that you have people like Meb and Joan to pray for you when you can't get past the bargaining and begging.

Jim doesn't worry much about how he prays. He's a "meat and potatoes" kind of pray-er, basic and straightforward. He goes to Mass as if he's collecting marbles in a jar up in heaven. While he falls asleep at the homily, I hang on every word, hoping to be enlightened, or at least be given a few practical pointers.

When, just before his surgery, Jim asks our priest friend to administer the "Anointing of the Sick," a Catholic sacrament, I know he is covering the bases of his religion. I am still suspicious and skeptical enough of the Church to wonder if this "hocus-pocus" does any good, but I'm also trying very hard to be on my best religious behavior and, of course, supportive of whatever will make Jim feel better. We go on Sunday afternoon, the day before the hospital procedure, to the rectory, where our friend offers us the prayers of this ancient rite of the Church. He prays for Jim, we pray together, and he blesses us in the name of God. I feel calm for the first time in a couple of days. I am beginning to understand that maybe I'm not alone in needing to hand over prayer to others in times of crisis.

There's a moment when you have no choice but to be brave and optimistic, and Jim and I have that moment as our eyes connect just as they wheel him out of the pre-op room for the angiogram that could turn into an emergency open-heart affair. My calm from the day before is short-lived and then gone altogether by the time I go off to the nearest waiting room, in this case a large corner seating area in an even larger front lobby. The room is very big and I feel very small in it, and suddenly exhausted.

Everything around me seems dim: the lighting, the muted colors, even the monotonous drone from electricity running through big and small machines. I am trying hard to pray well, but I realize I don't know what that means. What exactly are you supposed to ask for? A miracle if you need one? Peace of mind for Jim, and for me? Thy will be done? I fell into old habits as I sat there waiting. If your father can die at fifty-four, who's to say your husband can't die at forty-seven? And although I could call upon my strong belief in a higher power, I was feeling intimidated by the "higher" part. It is what it is. I have no control. God already knows the outcome. How can prayer do one iota of good for me now?

The cardiologist interrupts my thoughts as he saunters into the waiting area. He's tall—really tall—and somehow that gives me comfort, seeing him walk toward me like some larger-than-life Biblical hero. He assures me that Jim is fine. The angiogram showed more than a 90% blockage of the left anterior descending coronary artery. A stent was put in place to hopefully fix the problem; we won't know for sure if it worked for six months. In his clinical explanation, the cardiologist kept referring to the "narrowing." Relieved, I said "Oh, so it wasn't serious." He looked taken aback by my naïveté, eyebrows raised. "This is what we call 'the widow maker,' because many people don't get symptoms: they just drop dead. Your husband is very lucky. Had he remained asymptomatic and you had gone to Italy as planned, I would put his odds of having a massive 'coronary' as 'very high' in the next two weeks." (Good grief, God, I didn't mean to think about *From Here to Eternity* literally!)

I believe God is the Widow Maker. This is as good a definition as any to remind me that we puny humans are not in charge. This experience taught me that faith must be exercised, and the best way to exercise it is to pray—however flawed those prayers may be. I'm hoping that God factors this in, especially for people like me. And I am very grateful to the people who prayed for Jim, and for me, when I could not.

A few months later, after the episode with Jim was all but over, I felt compelled to research prayers and praying. I came across the one short prayer that I could have used from Anne Lamott: "Help me, help me, help me and thank you, thank you, thank you." I put this at the top of my prayer list for the next time—only when the next time came just a month later, I realized that it wasn't the right prayer at all.

It's still 1999. Joan's son David has survived a near fatal heart "attack" and, in January, had open-heart surgery. The Hill family moved to Boston in August and Jim survived his heart crisis in September. Other than the stigma of heart disease and a few daily pills, he was going to be fine too. Meb, Joan, and I thought we could finally get back to our Chase—but as it turned out, real life had other plans.

6

Fear of Flying

When you come to the edge of all the light you know,
and are about to step off into the darkness of the unknown,
faith is knowing one of two things will happen:
there will be something solid to stand on or you will be taught how to fly.

—Edward Teller

JOAN

Katie overestimated my prayer abilities, but it was good to know that someone believed in me. I had been feeling really unlucky because, in the month before David's diagnosis, I had received a rash of bad news from some of my closest friends. There was Nancy, my best friend from high school and college, who wrote to tell me about her breast cancer. Then I received an e-mail from Paul, another friend with another cancer. And out of nowhere, my dear friend Jack was found comatose and brain-dead. I was still reeling from the shock of these crises when the devastating circumstances of David's diagnosis confronted us.

As a rule, I am not someone who routinely asks for help. I much prefer the stoic approach of dealing with life on my own. Yet I found myself willing to ask for assistance. I couldn't possibly pray fairly for all of the people I cared about. How could I prioritize them or give them equal time?

As I drove past the church rectory on my way home one morning, I had an idea. I saw our parish priest, Father Declan, crossing the parking lot. I thought he would certainly know how to pray effectively for more than one cause. I needed to focus my prayers on my son with a clear conscience, and the last thing I needed was to add a healthy dose of Italian-Catholic guilt on top of everything else that was going on.

I pulled up next to him, asked if he had a moment, and described my dilemma. Instead of instantly agreeing to pray for those I cared about as I had thought he would, he did a strange thing. Right there in the parking lot where I had accosted him, he prayed and blessed me! I didn't want that—I had wanted him to take over for a while.

As I listened, I heard him ask God's blessing to provide me with serenity and the ability both to cope and to pray. It took me a long time to understand that what he did that day was far more valuable than what I had wanted. He prayed for my faith; he must have known I would need it.

Meb was still off investigating mystics and paranormal events, things not even remotely in my comfort zone. The Internet had provided her with a wealth of bizarre information, and she was really into St. Maximinus of Micy and people praying for help to minuscule body parts of saints. I thought that was disgusting; but since we had decided that our research should take us along on our individual journeys and not on a group tour, Katie and I listened skeptically, wondering just where this road would lead our fearless friend and how we would ever get her back to focusing on what we thought was important.

At one meeting, Meb told us about a number of mystical women she had encountered in her reading. "My favorite," she said, "is St. Julian of Norwich."

Julian was not someone any of us had ever heard of before, but she was apparently known to say "Trust in God, and every sort of thing will be all right."

While this resonated strongly with Meb and her own deep-seated desire for peace of mind, Katie had a really hard time with this kind of philosophy and wondered about the reverse: if every sort of thing is not all right, does that mean you didn't trust in God? Though Meb said it to me often enough over the next weeks and months, we both realized just how much more easily it was said than done. As time passed, everything fell into place in its own way. Nancy's cancer was treated, Paul's was removed, David survived; tragically, Jack never woke up.

I shared with Katie and Meb the incredible feeling of peace that had transformed me on the morning of David's surgery—when I realized that I really did have to give up control and completely trust in God. Only then would "every sort of thing be all right." I should have been a raving maniac in the waiting area outside the operating room for eight hours, which seemed like forever, while I continued not-knowing whether David would live or die. Instead, I was quite calm—by my standards, even serene. It was remarkable and, as my friends well know, most uncharacteristic.

As the months passed and we moved across the country, I went back to my old and comfortable ways. While I pray regularly, thanking God for the gifts that surround me in my family and friends, my more cynical side keeps surfacing. Can prayer really change the outcome, or is everything predetermined? How does it work, and why? It is far easier to think that everything is all prearranged, including the part where God anticipates our prayers and manipulates the result accordingly. I labored over this as Jim was diagnosed, Katie and Jim's marvelous trip canceled, and his angioplasty under way. I prayed, even though I wondered how my prayers from three thousand miles away could really help. How do you tap into the power of divine intervention? I hoped one of my old Wise Guy friends, Gottfried Wilhelm Leibniz, was right. I found comfort in his notion that God, being omniscient, knew what the best possible world would be. Being good, He always willed it, and, being omnipotent, He possessed the power to bring it into existence. I was always taught to pray, and that if we did, God would listen. But I berated myself because I seemed to possess an inability to stay constant in the belief that God cares and is willing to become involved in our individual lives. I want to believe Leibniz when he tells us that God works miracles, not "in order to supply the wants of nature, but those of grace." Like our parish priest, I want to understand that a prayer is a plea for grace and an invitation to the Divine to grant us strength.

I wondered whether my resurfacing cynicism could actually be due to my miracle research. I had come across so many non-believers—did they know something I didn't? This was not a good time to have this particular philosophical conversation with Katie, because, after all these months of miracle-chasing, I understood her well enough to know that she was having her own difficulty facing these same issues. The last thing she needed was a Doubting Thomas within the ranks of her close friends, and I was someone she thought prayed well—little did she know.

I was fascinated with a book from 1884 titled *A Dictionary of Miracles,* which came complete with illustrations; the author belittles the miracles that occurred throughout the ages as being repetitive and consequently make-believe. Depending upon who was in power at the time, many of a saint's accomplishments may or may not have been real. No big surprise there—I remembered some years ago when the Catholic Church revised its list of saints. Among those purged was St. Christopher, who, while not one of my favorites, was certainly the favorite of my father, who spent too much time on the road. Christopher was the patron saint of travelers, stemming from the legend that he had carried the Christ Child on his shoulders to cross a wide stream. Before we knew it, St. Christopher went from car dashboards to out the window—except in our car, where my father believed in covering all his prayer bases, including ones attached to the dashboard with magnets.

I had reverted back from the belief of trusting in God, which I had felt with so much immediacy, to my former state character-ized by uncertainty and a driving need to be in control. Talk about control. Remember what the year leading up to the new millennium was like? It was madness: fears of computer horror shows, tales of the end of the world; doom and gloom everywhere. I, on the other hand, figured that if the end was near, we should leave this world celebrating. And I had lots of friends who thought so too—Meb, Katie, and their families among them.

We decided to splurge and have a celebration that would long be remembered. Seven couples and sixteen kids armed with golf clubs, tennis racquets, swimsuits, and dancing shoes would spend the New Year in Pebble Beach, California. It made leaving Boston easier, knowing that we would soon be back among friends in order to enter the new millennium together. After the craziness surrounding our move, with kids in three different schools and a husband with a new job, my needs were simple—I just wanted to keep my sanity and get rid of the flowery wallpaper in our new house. A party among friends was just what the doctor ordered, and deliberation over prayer took a backseat.

And so, as I was packing up the grief and trauma of the past year, I was able to focus instead on the many blessings that had occurred with Jim, as well as David and Elizabeth's great progress and good health. But as Katie frequently reminds me, real life has its own plans, and my focus on life's many blessings was short-lived. This time, it is a lump in my breast. It isn't a muscle from my pre-move exercise regimen, and it isn't one of the familiar, annoying cystic bumps that come and go like old friends. This one is different. I am forced, once again, to recognize that I am not in control. I thought of Eric the shaman and his changed affect, his admonition to seek medical care. I need to pray, and preferably without the distraction of that nagging question dancing wildly through my brain—Will this really help, or not? I want to believe, to have faith, to know that "every sort of thing will be all right." I desperately want to find the elusive sense of peace that transformed me only months ago. I know it is possible. But why is it so hard?

The night before my surgery to remove the lump, as my six-year-old falls asleep in my arms, he tells me that you can talk to people in heaven with your heart. My daughter, now eleven, after a moment's quiet meditation, asks "Do you have cancer?"

"I hope not," I tell her as honestly and calmly as I can.

Over these last twelve months, I have been worn down by the emotional roller coaster I have been on. Though I am exhausted, I am reminded that in the opening of Pandora's box (if Katie, Meb, and I really opened it; I know we didn't mean to), and amid the escape of the horrors of the universe—which in our case seemed to bring trouble to those we love—the gift of hope also escaped. It is hope that I hold in my heart, which allows me to believe that divine intervention is not only possible, it truly exists.

I thought Meb would be proud of the number of excuses I can come up with to rationalize the fact that I can't be sick. I call her to explain: "I couldn't have a real problem; I am too young, too healthy, and far too chicken to have to deal with anything as serious as cancer. Besides, Mebby," I find myself whining, "it doesn't seem right. Haven't we just lived through a medical dilemma dramatic enough to last well into the next millennium?"

As I dress in the early-morning darkness for what will be my first surgery since having my tonsils out at age three, I pray to be delivered from any harm. Yet I can't quiet the immense fear I feel. The biopsy has to be negative; I can't possibly have breast cancer. I try hard to block out the concerns of my children, husband, and friends and really communicate with God. What have I learned in my miracle chase? I truly do believe in a very real way that there is a plan. I also believe that there is someone at the other end who is listening and looking out for me. I am not alone. I am really hoping that Leibniz is right, especially about the whole omnipotent thing and God's ability to make things be okay. Please, let that be true. . . .

Unfortunately, I find out that rationalizing only gets you so far, and in two short hours my life changes forever. The biopsy results are horrible. The diagnosis is not one I thought I could ever receive, or at least not yet. The cancer is invasive and the tumor is a large one. They tell me it is unlikely that the cancer is confined to the breast, and a mastectomy, lymph-nodal resection, and aggressive chemotherapy are likely all in the near future. I am in agony, not knowing if the cancer has already spread to my liver, lungs, or bones. For the first time, I feel my own mortality.

Again, I find myself relying on the strength of friends and family to ask God for help and to not let this signal a rapid death sentence. Even though I have moved so far away from the friends I lived with for over a decade, they send flowers, food, and good wishes. I am certain that heaven is barraged with their requests, thoughts, and prayers for me. They get together to support each other and share their hopes and fears. My new neighbors are wonderful, as they too help me while they drive my carpool route and pick up some of my other responsibilities. A feeling of peace begins to seep through. I feel less alone, less vulnerable. I feel the strength of their belief, their conviction that something good can result from all this. Slowly, I am able to pray, and I begin to believe that "every sort of thing will [actually] be all right." I know now that belief in miracles is not ethereal, not "out there somewhere"; it lives inside you and requires faith, whatever the outcome. Little did I realize that the miracle chase, once an intellectual and spiritual odyssey, was fast becoming a tool for my own survival.

I see more doctors and agree to be scheduled for surgery as soon as possible. I'm trapped in a maelstrom of life-threatening decisions. I can't decide which surgery to have. Should I undergo another lumpectomy and hope they find clear margins, or just schedule their recommended mastectomy? I don't even know whether I should have the new, less-invasive procedure to determine whether or not the cancer has spread to my lymph nodes. With surgery only hours away, I still have no idea what to do.

Sometimes knowing too much, as I did after twenty-five years in the healthcare field, is dangerous. I am torturing myself. After thinking about canceling the surgery altogether, I come to a decision: I opt for surgery, combining another lumpectomy with the most aggressive lymph-node resection possible in order to verify the extent of the spread of cancer. I need to know without question. I owe that to my six-year-old. I need to do whatever it takes to be here for him. For, like Monica with Augustine and Meb with Elizabeth, Gregory, my youngest, that free-spirited and sensitive child, needs me to run interference for him until he can do it on his own. I feel at peace. I have made the right decision and can finally talk to God with my heart.

On the day before Thanksgiving, my favorite holiday and my birthday that year, the oncologist called with mixed news from the surgical results. The margins were not clear. There was cancer pretty much everywhere within my breast. Mastectomy was the only option. But to his surprise, all my blood tests were normal, and the lymph nodes, all twenty of them, were cancer-free.

This changes the picture dramatically. While the weeks after my initial diagnosis were filled with scenarios of doom and gloom, now chemotherapy is for prophylactic purposes: a security blanket to be sure no nasty cancer cells escape only to cause trouble later. I can live with that. The hospital calls to schedule the mastectomy on December 7, and I'll be discharged cancer-free on December 8, the Feast of the Immaculate Conception—a celebration for the Lady of Bernadette's vision and the subject of the shrine of Lourdes. Every sort of thing will be all right.

Easy for me to say. I was just the one making decisions and taking care of business. Meb had the harder job—she was trying to take care of me. She came to Boston to provide moral support as I experienced what she knew would be hard for both of us. We had each faced near-fatal catastrophes with our first-born children and would easily have traded places with them if it meant they wouldn't have to suffer. But now it was one of us. Somehow the upcoming millennium didn't hold the same promise, the same beckoning spirit that we had anticipated together for such a long time.

Just as a piece of fabric has a different look and feel depending upon which side you see, Meb has a different view of our time together. The good news is that I had gotten nowhere in getting the ugly flowery wallpaper in my bedroom removed, but Meb had no problem in telling the paper-hangers that her friend had cancer and was going to be sick for a long time, so the ugly stuff in her room had to be changed quickly or they would be responsible for her feeling even worse! While it was probably true, I never would have used terms that were quite so blunt. That is the beauty of your friends: they protect you in ways you would never protect yourself. And in doing so, you all feel better.

7

GOING THE DISTANCE

And I hold that when God works miracles,
He does not do it in order to supply the wants of nature but those of grace.
Whoever thinks otherwise, must needs have a very mean notion
of the wisdom and power of God.

—G. W. Leibniz

MEB

I wanted to be in Boston, but couldn't picture how I'd arrange my life in order to do it. After Joan's diagnosis, at one of our miracle phone meetings, it seemed like she and Katie were getting wrapped up in miracle minutiae that didn't matter, at least compared to Joan's cancer. I only half-listened to the account of a miracle Katie found written up in *The Decline and Fall of the Roman Empire*, where a group of believers had their tongues cut out at the behest of the village chief, but kept right on talking. It was a "find," to be sure, since it's an important book—required reading in some history classes—and certainly not a place we expected to find the description of an African miracle.

Still, I couldn't stop thinking about Joan, wishing I could take her to doctors' appointments or sit with her through tests. I worried that she was blowing off the "cancer thing," as she called it, minimizing the seriousness of the illness and, in a sense, minimizing herself. She was too important in my life for me to let things go without saying something. After our meeting, I called her back to ask what kind of support she had in Boston, point-blank: was she able to find a friend to be there for her? Joan said she really didn't need anyone; her mother was there to help with the kids and she wasn't sick or anything.

"Oh, for crying out loud," I practically shouted. Knowing that whole "I'm fine and I don't really need anything right now" routine myself, I saw through her like a soul sister would.

"I don't want anyone here worrying about me," she explained.

"I will worry about you no matter where I am, Joan. Should I come?"

There was a long pause. "Well, if you really are going to be anxious and worry, I don't want that. Might as well come and worry here, then."

Getting coverage for the kids took guts, creativity, and intention. The truth is that on some level, it panicked me to leave them; it seemed like something always came up, and I was fearful I'd receive the call that a catastrophe had happened while I was away. My family support systems were limited to a husband who traveled four days a week, and parents and in-laws with schedules of their own. Yet Joan really had bailed my heart out of so many sad and anxious moments that I was determined to go.

Boston Logan is a crazy airport, apparently forever under construction. Joan picked me up and, after some creative and circuitous driving, we headed toward her new house north of Boston. We laughed as we drove through Salem, the home of the infamous witch trials (if they only knew what *we* were up to!), through the town where she grew up, past the estates of the Cabots, and the smaller mini-Cabot's, as I would call them, carriage houses turned into mansions in their own right. Finally, we drove into the park-like entrance to Joan's new colonial home. Impressive. It was new construction in an old part of the country. It felt like Joan had jumped into a universe I knew nothing about.

The warmth inside was all Joan, however. Like a mother ready to give birth, she wanted her nest ready, and I understood her need to leave everything the way she thought her family would like it—just in case. She gave me jobs to help her work through her To Do list (which was also—Impressive). Joan was focusing on the details. I knew that crossing things off the list allowed her to maintain a focus on the positive, on making progress in spite of everything, as well as a way to maintain a semblance of control when so many things were beyond her reach. I stood at the ready, determined to help her get it all done before she went into surgery.

Joan has a plant in her sunroom that a friend had sent as a house-warming gift. In the wake of the chaos left by her early days in Boston, what with the kids needing to be set up in new schools, boxes waiting to be unpacked, and doctors' appointments looming on the horizon, the plant has lost its lush greenhouse color and is looking pretty pathetic. Joan knows I have a green thumb, so she asks me to take care of the plant. She is worried it could die.

"Joanie," I say, "for it to live, you have to cut it back." Joan leaves me alone in the sunroom with the shears. She can't bear to watch.

Any gardener worth her salt knows that pruning is an art. Just like a surgeon, we must take out what is dead, cut out what is endangering the plant's vitality, and try to keep the aesthetic in mind. It takes a gardener to be able to see the plant cut back to its essence and imagine it full and lush in six months.

The imagery is not lost on either of us.

By the way, this whole prophylactic chemotherapy thing is absolutely Joan rewriting history into her story. Katie and I sure don't remember heaving a big sigh of relief when she told us her foolproof cancer-fighting strategy, and you would think it would be something we would remember. But that's okay; Joan's reign as the Queen of de Nile is safe with me. I know this about her, and I let her have her defense.

What I am having a hard time with is Joan's crazy schedule. I am exhausted, flying around with her in her bright red Volvo, and I have only been in Boston a couple of days. Yesterday, we were almost thrown out of a fancy, proper wig store for laughing too hard. We had hopped in her car, traveling at Joan-speed to the heart of Boston, where the historic brownstones are. Here on Newbury Street, the Rodeo Drive of Boston, the homes speak of elegance, affluence, style, and architecture. Iron black railings surround small, manicured gardens, and the solid wooden doors at the top of large stone steps suggest a lifestyle far different than my California Casual. Pulling up outside the shop, we barely can find this small, quiet establishment hidden away in this prominent neighborhood. So like Joan: somehow she knows that this is *the* place to purchase a Cancer Patient Wig.

The entrance to the wig shop is intimidating to both of us; but once inside, we are determined to make the most of it. I make Joan try on several wigs (something she really doesn't want to do). We try to find something to replace the long, beautiful dark hair that has been a part of her since high school and which she will probably lose.

Before you know it, we are laughing hysterically, assigning accents to wigs, even dancing around the counters. I am speaking with a Swedish accent, wearing a blond "do," when we hear a delicate throat-clearing sound. Apparently we are way too loud and having way too much fun. The two of us quiet down, but we burst out laughing again when Joan tries on a long, black Cleopatra wig. The squeaky, uptight owner now clearly notices our lack of Bostonian Decorum and chastises us, even though the place is completely empty. "Dear Ladies. If you cannot conduct yourself appropriately, I shall be forced to ask you to leave."

We feel as though Sister Mary Meanie has found a second calling as the Wig Lady, selling high-end wigs to cancer patients. Perhaps we are acting a little schoolgirlish; but damn, a girl has to have some fun, especially if she thinks she could die.

The next day, Joan and Gene rush off to their lawyer, not that the timing has anything to do with Joan's surgery that very afternoon. "It just worked out this way," Joan shrugs, as if one has surgery every afternoon. They are getting their legal documents in order; I guess it had to be moved to the top of the never-ending To Do list. On the way to the hospital, they drop me off at the Boston Museum of Fine Arts to fend for myself. I wander around, mostly in the gift shop. I check out the books and think about buying presents for the kids. Then I sit down in the café, overwhelmed by all Joan is going through. For the first time since I've come to Boston, I am afraid for her. No wonder she keeps moving so fast with errands and decisions and day-to-day existence. There is no time to feel afraid, just time for the next and the next and the next. She is unstoppable, like the uncontrolled cycle of the cancerous cells within her, going on and on until the turning point, when the surgeon will extract the terror of the cancer growing within her and she will be forced by the sheer insult to her body to rest—to stop.

This rush makes me feel so far away from the peace of chasing miracles. The fact that the small church Joan and I wanted to pray in yesterday was locked did not escape our notice. I understand that there is a part of Joan that is both sealed off and wished for at the same time. It is as though she wants to look and is afraid to look, needs to rest and is afraid to rest. How can I best support her? If I comment on the bind Joan is in, will she feel more confined, more helpless? As I sit there, I make a mental note of all that is good—her home, her family and friends, their love; and simultaneously, I find that I am thinking about the things Joan already has had to change, or leave behind, or give up in the last year.

I decide that I will leave the personal and psychological commentary for another time. I will just be myself with her. Back at her house, when this is over, we will copy over the notes from our miracle research onto our index cards, a silent testimony to the future, to hope, and to the belief in miracles that we had once spent so much time pursuing. For Joan, I pray for the miracle that would make the cancer go away. For both of us, I pray for the miracle of peace and the sense of being at home within ourselves, no matter where we are.

Joan's surgery becomes the turning point, where the three of us stop and look across a vast, imaginary line that heads both back in time and forward to the future. With her illness upon us so soon after the life-threatening emergency with Jim, we considered that we might be in defiance of some greater force and have some kind of black cloud hovering over us. We wondered if it was a kind of cosmic trick warning us to stay away from the Divine. Perhaps we were being sent a message, telling us to "Go back." "Do not enter." "You are entering the forest of *no* return." Or like the warning over the doorway to Hell that Dante saw before he entered, a more ominous "Abandon hope, all ye who enter here."

After I got back to California, we had a few phone meetings in which we honestly talked about quitting, something not one of us does, or at least does lightly. Joan thought the "death by miracle" theme she uncovered in her Wise Guy search had come too close for comfort and wasn't funny any more. Katie was inclined to agree. I thought chasing miracles was frivolous when looking at death's door. Together, we realized that we could either abandon our pursuit of miracles entirely, or acknowledge that our chase had become much more urgent and immediate.

C. S. Lewis of Narnia fame seemed to have been here before us:

> So it is a sort of Rubicon. One goes across; or not.
> But if one does, there is no manner of security against miracles.
> One may be in for anything.

In ancient Rome, a small river, the Rubicon, flowed into the Adriatic Sea. Protocol demanded that when invited into Rome, heads of state could cross the river, but their armies could not. In an act of defiance that changed history, Julius Caesar marched his army across the river. He told himself he would "conquer or die." Once he crossed the Rubicon, there could be no turning back, and his fate—and perhaps the fate of ancient Rome as well—was sealed. The effect of the miracle in each of our lives became our own personal Rubicon. And like Caesar before us, we found there could be no turning back.

Part Four

CHASING BEYOND

Everything is laid out for you.
Your path is straight ahead of you.
Sometimes it's invisible, but it's there.
You may not know where it's going.
But you have to follow that path.
It's the path to the Creator . . .
It's the only path there is.

—CHIEF LEON SHENANDOAH

8

A Quantum Leap of Faith

For the scientist who has lived by his faith in the power of reason,
The story ends like a bad dream. He has scaled the mountains of ignorance;
He is about to conquer the highest peak; as he pulls himself over the final rock,
He is greeted by a band of theologians who have been sitting there
for centuries.

—Robert Jastrow, *God and the Astronomers*

KATIE

Meb's right: I had felt a black cloud following us around. Had the three of us forgotten our place in the universe as "innocent" bystanders and stirred up some cosmic dust in the process? Joan's diagnosis frightened me. Never mind that there was a greater cataclysmic cloud predicted to be hovering over the whole earth as Y2K headed our way. Here we were, at the dawn of a new millennium, replete with dire predictions about the end of the world—and Joan has cancer. You have got to be kidding me. If it weren't that life kept moving, and me with it, I would have hibernated the rest of the winter, refusing to come out until the coast was clear. As it was, Joan, Meb, and I had made plans along with some other families to celebrate the turning of the millennium at Spanish Bay, a resort in Pebble Beach, California. We would ring in the New Year and face whatever the future brings together, Armageddon and cancer included.

In spite of the sponge-like way I seemed to be soaking up all the reports of doom and gloom, Spanish Bay is still Spanish Bay. Even on any old day, it gulps me into its magic like a thirsty sailor. We arrived on the afternoon of New Year's Eve. As Jim and I checked in, Laura and Allie stood near the enormous Christmas tree in the center of the lobby, looking up at the twinkling lights and down at the moving model train as it circled the base. The bustle around the lobby for the extravaganza that evening lent an air of excitement. The girls led us out of the lobby to our favorite spot, one of the large outdoor fireplaces, where we stayed warm against the winter chill and waited for our friends to arrive. We sat on one of the benches that faced the ocean some two hundred yards in the distance, hailed a waiter for warm blankets, and ordered hot drinks. It was our tradition to wait for the serenade of the bagpipe player at sunset, and we were lucky to have found a seat.

Meb, Bob, and some other friends rounded the corner of the hotel, returning from a walk on the beach, kids skipping and straggling behind them, and squeezed in around our bench. As the sun began to set and the bagpiper began to play, the kids ran around a stretch of grass between us and the beach, and Meb and I commiserated about Joan.

"The woman is amazing—I can't believe they are still coming," I tell Meb, though I am selfishly thrilled they are. So like Joan: breast removed, check; decide on most aggressive course of chemotherapy, check; first chemo treatment not until January, check; therefore, hair will not have fallen out, check; squeeze in a family trip to California to see old friends, check.

"I think she's actually more concerned about the temporary loss of her hair than the permanent loss of her breast . . . try and psychoanalyze that one, Meb," I continued.

"All I really know is that she needs us, all of us; she wants to come back to what's familiar, and that's why she's coming," Meb replied thoughtfully.

Joan knows how to make an entrance, that's for sure. As the last rays of the sun dipped below the ocean's edge, the Hill family arrived. I waited to give Joan a long hug as they were immediately surrounded, children included, eager to welcome them. I realized then how relieved I was to see Joan looking the same as the day she had left, and suddenly I understood why keeping her hair was so important to her. You would never have known what this woman had just gone through or is up against in the coming year. She seemed to sparkle like the Christmas tree, clearly in possession of the wisdom to enjoy the moment, and she managed to pull us all along with her.

The merriment on New Year's Eve was real, captured in a photograph in the waning hours of 1999: Joan in a black sheath dress, hair long, dark and youthful; Meb as happy as I'd seen her, wearing her signature green—even she seemed to be living in the moment; and me in dark blue laughing between them. We were in a cocoon for a few short days and happy to be there.

Coming home from our wonderful time at Spanish Bay, the new century hit like a lingering hangover. Joan began her chemotherapy, and I made my own plans to visit Boston with my daughter Allie in tow over the Presidents' Day weekend. Joan picked us up at the airport in the beginning of a snowstorm and drove through the swirling wind, seemingly oblivious to the perils of the road. By the time we got to her house, the snow was piling up and quite beautiful, making the warm fire Gene had started all the more welcoming. We sat by the fireplace, sipping glasses of wine, as our children made snowmen outside, a moment so peaceful that I could almost forget the steady onslaught of worry that had piled up over the past six months. We caught up on the kids, schools, sports, and husbands. And then we caught up on the chemo, how it made Joan feel, how much longer it would go on.

"I have a new 'stick-on boob'," Joan suddenly declared, laughing as she saw the shocked expression on my face. "It can actually be stuck on anywhere, creating an opportunity for an interesting bedroom game," she continued, clearly pleased with the effect her announcement was having on me.

I raised my glass to her, not sure what else to do, and finally burst out laughing as our glasses clinked in the air.

And so it went throughout Joan's six-month ordeal: her sense of humor remained intact, and her bravery only wavered when her beautiful hair began to fall out by the handful. As far as our chase was concerned, we may have crossed the Rubicon, and we may have decided not to turn back, but we were not exactly marching along in perfect rhythm as I imagine Caesar and his Roman soldiers had.

Still, the unintended break from the original pace of our miracle research and writing was a good one for me. As Joan has pointed out, thinking is a prerequisite when you're researching something like miracles. But too much thinking can make your brain feel overloaded. For months after my visit, as Joan endured chemo treatment after chemo treatment, I was in mental limbo—stuck, unable to go forward or backward. I just couldn't write, or think, about miracles. Would she beat the cancer? "Please, God, Joan needs to beat the cancer." (My prayers weren't getting any more eloquent, but at least I was praying.) All the while, I was still anxious about Jim, every time he was late back from a run, or from work, or even from the grocery store. Reality and paranoia make for an ugly combination.

June finally arrived; the chemical assault on Joan's body was over. Somehow this made it easy for me to hop on the cancer-is-gone bandwagon, even though I knew she was just beginning the will-it-come-back waiting game. I was in need of light, as in "feather light," or some joy. *Joy:* now there's a word. Fortunately, I can find whole scoops of joy in the company of my children; and that summer, with my brain on autopilot, I slowly returned to my natural state of contentment. The summer included another visit to see the Hills, this time the focus on family, the beach, and glorious sunsets.

The day before we headed home to California, Joan organized a day at the beach for our five children, dads in charge, and whisked me away to a charming little coffee shop where we spent the better part of the afternoon recapping where we were with the book and what to do next.

"Meb's coming with her family in a couple of weeks, and she and I will pick up where you and I leave off. Then, when the kids are all back in school, we can resume our usual meetings." The maestro was back, and our miracle discussions returned.

The school year begins with my daughter Laura at a new high

school, and I feel new again too. Not to mention that Jim and I are going to Italy at the end of the month, the same trip that had been canceled the year before. One late September day, while driving to San Francisco to meet Laura's volleyball team at a tournament, I have that feeling of the world being right side up once again. The day is spectacular, as only San Francisco can be this time of year—Joan says I'm a tad biased about this—and the traffic is moving at the speed limit, even though the evening commute is underway. As the freeway curves around directly into the sun, I reach for my sunglasses. Suddenly, I hear the sound of a truck coming up on my left, fast. What happens next is a blur. An object catapults straight at me, crashing through my windshield. The splinters of the shattered glass fly at my face and into my mouth. For a split second I think maybe I have been impaled and feel no pain. Somehow I make my way safely to the next exit, spitting as I go, terrified of swallowing the glass I feel in my mouth and relieved that I can still see. After pulling over to the side of the road, I find the two-foot-long metal pipe that has landed between my seat and the door.

Other than minor facial and mouth cuts, scratched sunglasses, and needing a tow truck, I am fine—on the outside. Later, the California Highway Patrol would tell me the truck must have hit the pipe in the freeway and sent it spiraling at 350 miles per second to have shattered the so-called bulletproof windshield of my car. A friend tells me that I must be like a cat with nine lives. I feel incredibly lucky, but also uncomfortable in my skin. Just as I was stepping out into the light, I am yanked back into the shadow. While I should be celebrating that my head is still attached, I am mostly cringing to think that a metal pipe has almost taken it off. I hate to be superstitious, but maybe we should have turned back—forget Caesar and the damn Rubicon.

So much for my return to thinking about chasing miracles; and no, I did not consider this to be one—just a stupid, random, completely out-of-my-control disaster in the making, and then a lucky miss. Or not—that's the thing with thinking too much. The thought that maybe there is some grand plan crept into my mind, or that maybe this was a rude reminder that the "black cloud" was still with us. Regardless, I fell into a funk that lasted for months. If you can't count on driving down the freeway without pipes blasting through your windshield, there's not a lot of comfort in getting up in the morning.

Funk or not, the accident did jump-start my mental batteries. I was back to thinking too hard and too much about the possibility of divine intervention, hoping for divine inspiration, and settling for a disquieting spiritual no-man's-land. I thought about an experience I'd had a few years before, when I attended a conference in Dallas for the Susan G. Komen Breast Cancer Foundation, an organization I'd been involved with for years. I took the opportunity to meet some old friends for dinner. They were the kind of Southern Christians who wore their religion a bit on their sleeve, which was a somewhat uncomfortable situation for a lapsed Catholic like me. During the course of our evening together, I told them my story. At the end, as they stared at me dumbfounded, I blurted out, "Why me? Why was I spared?" Maybe these thank-the-Lord-God people would be able to help me out.

"Did you ever think," one of my friends offered, "that this miracle was meant to save your soul, not just your life? Maybe the experience was meant to force you to face your skepticism of God and the spiritual nature of things." A miracle, as ransom for my soul—at the time, it was a thought I hadn't considered.

The pipe flying through the windshield propelled me, once again, out of my false sense of security and forced me to face my overriding skepticism, a state of mind that makes for some convoluted thinking when you believe miracles can and do happen. In spite of the obvious disconnect this presents for me, accepting a personal miracle takes it one step further, conflicting in an almost insurmountable way. With the absence of divine intervention in the gutters of human wretchedness, it is difficult to be a cheerleader for your own miraculously saved life. Wise Guy C. S. Lewis seemed to understand, as he wrote "the 'real world' when you come back to it is so unanswerable."

For me, the "real world" could be found on the front page of the morning newspaper: murder and mayhem, the usual fare. Sometimes random accidents or natural disasters make the headlines; they come out of nowhere and in a split second or two you're either dead or saved. And what do the experts with the most advanced degrees from the most prestigious universities have to say about this world of ours? Turns out that a significant percentage of scientists conclude that there is no God—what you see is what you get. No meaning or purpose to this bag of bones we call "human," no afterlife, no miracles; not even a really smart space alien behind the action. While Joan had moved on to further explore miracles and their place in world religions, and Meb was in the thick of college applications for Liz, I decided to pursue a little history of science to find out how we got ourselves in this mess. I had to find out what these scientists knew that I didn't.

Ironically enough, it seems to have begun with the Enlightenment. All those Wise Guys were busy thinking about more than miracles as they advanced our knowledge of the natural world. For example, Ben Franklin's discovery around 1750 that lightning was not, in fact, a form of divine communication; and a hundred years later, give or take, Charles Darwin dispensed all previous notions about Adam and Eve and the rather speedy creation of the world—so much for serpents, apples, fig leaves, catastrophic falls from grace, and resting on the Seventh Day. (Not that mothers ever got to rest on the seventh day anyway.) If you lived in the nineteenth century, this unraveling of "how the world works" was very big news. It's not much of a jump in reasoning to conclude that practically all mysteries would ultimately come to be explained scientifically. God developed a serious credibility problem—kind of like "the Emperor has no clothes" in the Hans Christian Andersen fairy tale. Next thing you know, there were questions about other biblical characters and stories, including Jesus and His miracles. Finally, a sizable leap of faith became required just to believe in God, *anybody's* God. Nietzsche's infamous one-liner summarized this period succinctly: "God is dead."

That's the problem with a simplistic or magical idea of God. I call Him the Santa Claus (SC) God. He's an older white man with a beard, capable of granting the wishes of a select constituency: those who believe in Him and follow His rules. He's actually SC with a dark side, because if you're not good, He can send fire and brimstone your way, and then you're dead. Once the newly "enlightened" were able to dispense with SC God, it seems they arrived quickly at the point where there was no God at all. Hard to believe these guys couldn't come up with anything (or any One) at all in SC's place. Instead, the pursuit of knowledge became the new God, each grand discovery sending us up one more rung on the ladder to our own personally orchestrated nirvana.

Then along came Albert Einstein and his theory of relativity, which inadvertently may have allowed God back in. In laywoman's terms, Einstein proved that there is no such thing as absolute Time. Time, that master-knot ruling all our lives, is not what it seems. There is no such thing as absolute Space either. Space and Time only exist relative to each other; one cannot exist without the other. Together, they form a space/time continuum, with time representing a fourth dimension. This is as simple as I can make it, and it still feels like a brain teaser. A fourth dimension? I find it hard enough living in three!

While I was trying to understand the implications of Einstein and his spark leading to a whole new way of evaluating the world, a miracle story from long ago captured my attention. The miracle at Fatima in Portugal is an unlikely story for me to focus on because, in contrast to Meb and Joan, I'm not a Mary devotee; and Fatima, like Lourdes, is a story of the Blessed Mary appearing to children. But I couldn't help myself.

When I was a child, my mother had us gather at random times to say the rosary on our knees, like in the middle of the upstairs hallway at ten o'clock in the morning before we could go out to play. My grandmother Alice (not the one who let me eat The Hamburger on Good Friday) had shared the story of the strange happenings at Fatima with my mom when she was a child, how the Blessed Mother had appeared to these three shepherd children and told them to say the rosary for peace in the world. I hated saying the rosary at random times and wanted desperately to tell my mother that the Blessed Mother didn't mean *her* children, but didn't think it would get me off my knees, just sent to my room. When my patient mother brought up Fatima when we were talking about our miracle chase, I didn't listen. And then she brought it up again. And again. I finally decided to check it out, because that's what you do when your mother keeps nudging you—proof that even I could learn something from Augustine; it's better to cave in when a mother nudges and save yourself a lot of trouble later on.

The miracle of Fatima involved more than fifty thousand witnesses, believers and nonbelievers alike, and a spectacular show from the heavens, predicted in advance and without any credible scientific explanation. I can get behind miraculous fireworks when even skeptics take notice. Ironically, it became the keystone of my current search, my own spiritual "angle of repose."

In 1917, Portugal, like the rest of Europe, was at war. Although the population was predominantly Catholic, an anti-clerical government was in charge and had banned the ringing of church bells, the wearing of clerical garb, and the celebration of religious festivals. On May 13 of that year, three children playing in a meadow in the small village of Fatima saw a strange light approach and hover above a nearby oak tree. The light transformed into a beautiful lady who spoke directly to them. She said she was from heaven and that they should not be afraid, and she asked them to pray for peace in the world. She also told the children she would come again at midday on the thirteenth of every month, for a total of six consecutive months, and promised to reveal who she was and why she had come.

Over the course of the next four months, news of the children's experience spread. On the thirteenth of each month, more and more people gathered in the meadow; but although these witnesses saw the enraptured peace on the children's upturned faces, none experienced the apparition themselves. Many reported hearing a muffled buzzing sound, sensed a dimming of the sun, and saw a small wisp of a cloud above the tree. Some heard a clap of thunder upon the apparition's departure and noticed that the upper branches of the oak tree leaned strangely to the east, the direction the children had pointed when the light departed. On one occasion, shimmering petals fell from the sky, dissolving as they hit the ground.

The lady of light continued to speak to the children during these visits. She told them to pray the rosary for peace in the world and for the souls of sinners. To their horror, on one visit she revealed a glimpse of Hell and made predictions regarding the end of World War I, the beginning of World War II, and the spread of communism. She asked the children to keep these revelations secret for a while. In return, they requested a sign so those who doubted their story might come to believe. In answer, she promised a great miracle on her final visit in October.

Their parents, the local priest, and other visiting religious representatives questioned the children extensively. Others ridiculed the children. Even Maria Rosa, the mother of Lucia, the oldest and the perceived ringleader, initially insisted that her daughter must be lying. By no means was there agreement that the apparitions were real. In addition, the religious fervor attached to the visions at Fatima presented a problem for the regional government. Led by a man openly hostile to the Catholic majority, who was determined that he not lose the upper hand in the fight to quash religious faith, he kidnapped the children to prevent further disturbance. Kept against their will, interrogated and threatened with death, the children still refused to deny the experience of the lady of light or to reveal the secrets she had told them. After two days, he sent the children home. The news of their treatment and refusal to yield to

Senhor Administrador's demands lent credibility to their story, and word of the apparitions spread even farther.

As the October date approached, there were fears that if the miracle did not occur, a hostile crowd would harm the children and their families. There were even rumors that a bomb would explode—not so farfetched an idea in time of war. The children themselves remained calm, certain of the lady's promise. October 13, 1917 dawned cool and stormy as an enormous crowd of more than fifty thousand people made their way to the Cova da Iria. Perhaps it was out of fear for her daughter that Maria Rosa went to the meadow for the first time that day. A heavy rain pounded through the noon hour, drenching the multitude. As in the previous months, a sphere of light was seen by many and came to rest over the lone oak tree. After several minutes, the light ascended into the sky and vanished. Throughout this interlude, the rain had continued to fall. At the moment the light disappeared, the rain stopped suddenly and the clouds dispersed, as if an invisible arm had yanked open heavy drapes. The sun dimmed and all eyes were able to stare at it directly. All of a sudden, the sun seemed to dislodge from its place in the heavens and began to spin rapidly, spewing the colors of the rainbow from jagged edges. Three times the sun "danced" in this way until the final "dance," when, with catastrophic speed, it began a dizzying spiral and terrifying plummet toward the thousands of people below. At the last instant, it disappeared, leaving behind the warmth and safety of the real sun, too brilliant to look at any longer. Although their clothes and hair had been soaked only minutes before, everyone was now completely dry.

There was widespread agreement from those present on what they had experienced that day. "Atheists, skeptics and liberal newspaper reporters" were included in the group of witnesses to the strange occurrences, and detailed descriptions were carried in the newspapers of the day. Maria Rosa was one of those who saw the sun's gyrations—and, what's more, she experienced an unusual, beautiful fragrance during the time of the lady's visit, the same fragrance that had overwhelmed her when her daughter brought her a tree branch from one of the lady's previous visits. She embraced her daughter's story and finally left her skepticism behind.

Not surprisingly, I relate to Maria Rosa and to the other skeptics in this story. If you aren't expecting something to be real, then your own preconceived notions are working against its being true. When you decide it *is* real, well, to me, it just carries more weight. Joan and Meb tell me that I don't fall into the "less is more" category where miracles are concerned. It's true—give me fireworks every time. And the Fatima miracle has tangible phenomena verified by thousands, which is evidence to hold up to the greatest skeptics of all: scientists who conclude that there is no God, and by extension, no such thing as a miracle.

With the Fatima story in mind, I can finish my own warp-speed version of the history of science. Nineteen-seventeen, neatly enough, falls right between Einstein's discovery of relativity in the early part of the twentieth century and the momentous discoveries that build on quantum theory in the 1920's. At the atomic and sub-atomic level, all those causal, deterministic, mechanistic laws of classical physics are contradicted. Three things come to light: first, matter at the atomic level possesses characteristics of both waves and particles, "wave-particle duality." Second, the nature of these particles is a statistical one, based on probable outcomes; yet their predictability is uncertain at the same time. And third, it is impossible to know both the momentum and the position of a particle without affecting it in some way. What you see is not what you get, and thus chance was added to the world of nature. What's more, the observer—you and I—become part of the reality; our participation in the world affects how the world works. Nature began tingling with mystery—we were no longer "just along for the ride." Quantum physics is revolutionary not only because it sparked the next great chapter in scientific discovery, but also because the rationalist could entertain once again the idea that Divinity may dance upon our shores.

"God does not play dice with the Universe" was Einstein's infamous reaction regarding the new physics. Certain that a future experiment would prove many of the implications of quantum physics wrong, he doctored his groundbreaking equation on the gravitational influences on the universe itself with a "correction factor" to manipulate the outcome of the original version of the equation, because that outcome showed the universe expanding – an expanding universe meant a beginning to Time, and introduced the possibility of a cause for that beginning. Einstein later called his behavior "the greatest mistake of my career," not because, I suspect, he had some religious epiphany, but because he was too great a scientist to waffle on his experimental integrity—along with the fact that, by that time, it was acknowledged by all physicists that the universe *is* expanding. Cosmologist Stephen Hawking gives us his version of "dice" in *A Brief History of Time* when he suggests the possibility that if the universe had no beginning, "What place then for a creator?" Nietzsche, to some, is very much alive.

Why does all this matter to me? While I find comfort in nature's inconsistencies and mystery, the strange events at Fatima have plenty of skeptics. We've all got our point of view, and it's not possible to claim absolute proof. Thankfully, that's not the point—or, at least, it's not *my* point. I just wanted to know if there was some wiggle room. I can't wrap my faith around total darkness. I realize that faith is more than an educated guess and less than knowing for sure. I want to be a thinking believer and take a leap of faith too. I like that—challenging, but grounded.

Nearly a year of thought and discovery had passed and summer was in the air once again before I was able to recapture the feeling I had right before the windshield came crashing in on me. I was driving to another volleyball game, this time to Berkeley, no highway involved and much closer to home. There must be more bumper stickers there than anywhere else in the country, and they still favor the anti-war, anti-establishment, peace sentiments of the sixties. It was here that I came across the one that will always be my favorite, the one that enabled me to imagine that God and I share the same sense of humor:

Nietzsche is dead.
—*God*

9

MAKING THE CONNECTION

We may climb the mountain from different paths,
but the view from the summit is identical for all.

—A SOURCE BOOK OF INDIAN PHILOSOPHY

JOAN

I love Katie's sense of the ironic. Her sense of humor is honest and straightforward: when she gets the joke, her free-spirited laugh is contagious. During our miracle mission, we were like sponges soaking up any information we could find about topics that intrigued us, and while Meb's eyes glazed over when listening to Katie expound on Fatima and Einstein, I thought it was fun to see Katie so animated and watch her mad-scientist side emerge. Usually Katie was the one teasing me about my interest in the whole "healing shrine" thing and about being, as she called it, a Mary fan. I guess I've always seen Mary as way more user-friendly than most of the male religious characters I've found. I am not so much a feminist as a practical realist. When Christ says to his mother "He is your son," indicating the disciple John, and to John "She is your mother" (John 19:26–27), I know who's in charge, and it isn't the son—it plays right into my need for control. But now Katie was the one leading the charge with Mary alongside strange scientific phenomena. She was finding relief from the conundrum she faced between skepticism and faith.

Not knowing much about Fatima other than it was in Portugal, I found Katie's description of the sun's dance intriguing, not so much because it happened, but because it made believers out of so many. Still, there really is no accounting for taste—I'll take healings over secrets any time. Katie found the fireworks at Fatima illuminating, but I've always preferred miracles in simpler circumstances. That's the beauty of miracles. While some of us are enthralled by a momentous event and see it as an affirmation of faith, others prefer the more down-to-earth message of practical assistance in times of woe.

It was not long after our Fatima discussions that I went for my first GYN visit since my cancer diagnosis. Though nervous, I was relieved to find that the physician, who had been referred by a friend, was a white-haired Irish delight. He put me instantly at ease, declaring that I should go to my grave an old woman, dying in my sleep. He advised me to view cancer as a thing of the past. I was delighted with his prognosis and found myself willing to give him a straight answer when he asked "So, what do you do?"

"Though I worked in healthcare my whole life, over the past few years I've been writing a book with two other women."

"Oh? On what?" he inquired.

"It's a book about miracles. Views of the philosophers, scientists, various religions, that type of thing."

"Really?"

"Yes." I smiled. "It's been great therapy."

He became quiet, and even in this short visit I knew this was uncharacteristic of him. A moment later, he grew serious, and the twinkling in his eyes took on a new hue. I panicked, thinking he had just found something to reverse his earlier pronouncement of good health.

Instead, he said, "You've just reminded me of something I haven't thought about for quite some time." The pause in our conversation was palpable.

He continued. "A number of years ago, I was asked if I would be willing to treat a woman from Europe who needed an operation. She wouldn't become one of my regular patients; she would come in, have the surgery, and leave."

This hardly seemed unusual, since he practices at a large teaching hospital and people often come from far away and then leave again after their treatment. Though I wondered what was coming next, nothing could have prepared me for where his story would take us.

"Prior to her surgery, I did the usual history and physical exam, and, speaking through an interpreter, I found out that she was a Portuguese nun. Everything went well, and it was not until she was leaving that I came to understand she was one of the three children who had seen the Blessed Virgin Mary."

He paused, seemingly lost in time, and then continued reverently. "At first, I didn't think too much about it, but then I realized I had been in the presence of someone who had seen Mary the Mother of God. I was in awe."

Blessed Mother—Portugal! To borrow one of Katie's favorite phrases, "You have got to be kidding me." Did you ever notice how you hear about something you'd never heard of before, and then suddenly it's everywhere?

Listening to him gave me goose bumps, which is bad enough in general and even worse when dressed in a hospital gown. Who knows why, but my first thought was of the popular movie *Six Degrees of Separation*, with its premise that everyone on earth can be connected to each other within six relationships. I thought of it as a reassuring, self-perpetuating system solidifying our place in the world.

Suddenly, the link between Katie, the one for whom Fatima had become the bridge between faith and skepticism, and Mary, the Mother of God, was way closer than arm's-length. Naïvely, I had assumed six degrees only worked for people, and was shocked to see it in our relationship to God as well. I was beginning to think we were not just "crossing" the Rubicon, but maybe we really were being "portered across" in some grand scheme.

I couldn't wait to tell Katie and Meb about the eerie coincidence with my new doctor. When we finally spoke on the phone, we agreed that we had learned more about people through the writing of this book than we would have in years as their friends or neighbors. There's an instant camaraderie with nearly everyone who asks about our Miracle Chase. Stories of coincidental meetings that changed lives, physical danger averted and thought to be a divine intervention, or just events that brought them closer to believing.

"So many people have, or know of, a miracle story," Meb interjected.

I agreed. "It seems, even when you're not expecting it, stories of the miraculous constantly come up. Last week, I took my mom to see a new doctor. He thought he was God's gift to orthopedics. Even he softened when my mother told him I was writing a book on miracles—I think she was trying to give me some credibility with this guy. And it worked, because while one minute he made no pretense of his disbelief in God (we both had the sense that he thought he *was* God), he visibly mellowed the next minute, describing how he had been overwhelmed by the power of Mother Teresa. He told us how the hair on the back of his head had stood straight up with the majesty of this small, sick woman, a patient at the hospital where he had trained. He pulled out the holy card he still carried in his wallet with her picture. I would have expected a laminated, card-sized copy of his medical school diploma or his license to practice medicine in his wallet, but a holy card of Mother Teresa—no way."

Meb commented on how odd it was that an atheist would believe in a saint. "It's pretty strange," said Meb. "Just shows you that she was really a powerhouse. If Mother Teresa could impress this guy, she could impress anyone."

"True. But I have another story, about a nicer guy, with the same kind of feeling. You know my friend Tony, who I talk about sometimes—the one I do so much fundraising with for our old high school. Shortly after his father's death, when I offered my condolences, he shared an amazing story with me. We didn't know each other very well then, but he explained to me how, one evening when he was leaving after his daily visit to see his comatose father, a nurse he had never seen before asked him to stay. She foretold that this would be the night of his father's passing. Her presence and under-standing helped Tony be at peace as they prayed at his father's bed-side. Despite his repeated attempts to locate her the next day, he couldn't find a record of her anywhere. This mysterious woman still haunts his thoughts."

"All these stories might not be miracles, though, and not everyone thinks that way," Katie commented. "But it really is amazing the things people tell us; it's like we've given them permis-sion to talk about something they usually aren't comfortable sharing with others."

Meb went further. "I wonder if we don't talk about miracles because we are hoping one day to understand, forget, or reconstruct them. So we don't want to share something we don't fully under-stand. Then time goes on and we rationalize the experience away."

I agreed. "Still, lots of people have told me that in baring their souls, they experience a new sense of freedom - recognizing that their lives intersected with divine providence."

Everywhere we turned, people were intrigued and honest-to-god interested, wanting to know what we were uncovering. Each of us heard heartrending stories of survival, like the one told by my daughter's close friend Katie, from Alaska, whose family had one such experience on a lonely highway during a sub-zero Arctic night. Until I went to Alaska, I had thought that the Rocky Mountains were remote. But Alaska is like Colorado on steroids: the mountains are bigger, the wildflowers are wilder, the weather is colder, and it's a lot more isolated with a lot fewer people. One particular weekend, in deference to the Alaskan winter, her parents had taken the unusual step of renting a new van instead of using their old car for a trip. As they headed home along a deserted highway in the Sterling Mountains, her mom got an urge to put on all four children's snow pants and jackets. Climbing into the back seat, she dressed them in their heavy clothing and then checked to be sure their seatbelts were secure. Moments after refastening her own seatbelt, a moose stepped onto the road in front of them and sent the car spiraling off the highway and rolling over into a ditch. Hanging upside down in a remote area, with no one around and no available coverage on their cell phone, they were stunned when, almost immediately, an arm appeared through the shattered driver's side window holding a cell phone. "I have a state trooper on the line; tell him you need help," a voice told Katie's father, Jon, handing him the phone. Shards of glass were everywhere, but the children were unscathed, protected by their down-filled snowsuits. As Jon gave the trooper the information, the man released the children from their upside-down seatbelts and led them through the snow to safety. Just then, a car with two women inside pulled over to the side of the road and piled the children in to keep them warm. When the parents finally made their way up the embankment after disentangling themselves from the wreckage of the van, they were relieved to find their children safe and squealing with joy, contented with the juice boxes and kid-friendly treats the women had provided. None of them had seen or heard another car, and the man who had saved them was nowhere to be found. When the state trooper took them to the nearest house to warm up, they were shaken from the effects of the crash, but mostly overwhelmed at having been rescued by their "very own guardian angel."

The stories we heard helped us keep going; there was something to this power, something that transcended the ordinary relationship we have with each other. We weren't a bit surprised when a 2000 *Newsweek* magazine poll found that over 80 percent of adults in the United States believed in miracles. An AARP poll in 2009 and a 2010 Pew poll of the millennium generation continue to confirm these findings.

While each of us was drawn to miracle stories, I was the one who was not so worried about their validity or truth, because who could really know? That was a problem for David Hume, the first significant anti-miracle Wise Guy, but not for me.

I wondered whether they did polls back in the eighteenth century, when Hume was outlining his four rationalizations against belief in miracles. I was curious about what people thought. After all my reading I was pretty certain that they would have been appalled that Hume would be so bold. I was still amused as I shared this thinking with Meb and Katie at one of our weekly phone meetings.

"Hume was an important guy," Meb acknowledged more seriously than I had anticipated. "Liz learned a lot about him in her Philosophy classes."

"Four rationalizations?" Katie interjected. "This I gotta hear."

"You'll like his first one, Katie. He argued there was a lack of discerning and competent witnesses to the miracles of Jesus. Sound familiar?" I chuckled.

"Second," I continued, "he believed that we humans are prone to exaggeration, making all miracle stories suspect. Okay, I might be guilty of exaggeration once in a while," I admitted. "But just as a joke, not about something important.

"Then he proposed that so-called miracles abounded only among ignorant and barbarous nations."

"That just about covers every nation," Meb remarked.

"And," I continued, "the reason I find most hysterical is that Hume actually thought miracles of rival religions canceled each other out! Where do people come up with this stuff? I don't understand it, but his essay 'Of Miracles' has received a huge amount of attention over the years—the point–counterpoint to Augustine, I guess."

I was making Meb and Katie crazy with my need to find out what everyone else was thinking before drawing my own conclusions. Katie wanted the abridged version. If she could find a rationale for miracles in the scientific world, she would be happy. Meb didn't have to explore, she just knew—and once Meb knows, she isn't the type who really cares what anyone else thinks. I guess that makes me the insecure one; but for someone like me who starts pondering the universe, that's okay. From my perspective, a bit of insecurity seems more than reasonable when it is God we are trying to understand.

I was finally ready to move on past the Wise Guys, to understand whether miracles had found a way to be encapsulated within other religions. I liked the notion that miracles could be a common thread, woven into the fabric of different systems of belief, and thought that the underlying miracle stories could tell us about the way others conceived of their God. I knew the Jewish tradition had miracles—just think of Moses and the sea. And I had just found out more than I ever wanted to know about the lengths Protestants went to disprove the miracles Catholics were so fond of investigating. But I had no idea about Eastern religions or even Islam. As it turned out, I found miracles present in every religion I explored.

In stories, we go outside ourselves. We learn from them; we find metaphors for life and guides for living. Stories allow us to put a framework around experiences we don't understand. And with the words "Once upon a time," we are transported to another place. So it was with the stories I was drawn to in my miracle search. While Katie wanted facts, I was okay with fiction.

I started with Native American legend as the basis for my search. Maybe it was because of the Native American artifacts Gene and I started collecting in the early days of our courtship, or maybe it was because Meb had come to one of our first miracle meetings full of enthusiasm with a story she had found on tape about letting go of grief in order to go on living. I'm glad I had been there when she told us the story of Ayonwentha, who I always knew as Hiawatha.

"Ayonwentha was a warrior of the Seneca tribe who married and left his family and former life behind to become a husband in another clan," Meb began paraphrasing the story for us.

"Life for the young married couple was good, and soon there were many beautiful children, all daughters, to make them content and happy. The children were so beautiful, so alive and vibrant, that the family attracted the attention of an elder of the tribe, a selfish, evil man who had a collection of wives. He approached Ayonwentha and demanded that his first daughter become one of his wives. Ayonwentha felt the man's evil nature and feared for his daughter's happiness and safety. He refused, and the evil man was furious. He wanted to see that Ayonwentha suffered for his refusal. One by one, the evil man used his magic and power and destroyed *all* of Ayonwentha's children as well as his wife, who died of grief.

"Ayonwentha left the village and journeyed for years in his own grief, walking as though blind, crashing into trees, falling into ravines, torn by the thorns and barbs of bushes, and going from freezing to burning with the changes of the seasons.

"Finally, Ayonwentha finds himself in front of a vast lake—a lake so vast, he cannot see its boundaries. He is now an old man and he makes his way to the edge of the silvery, silent lake. The moon's shape is reflected like a wise woman's face, smooth and unwrinkled on the surface of the lake. All is stillness. He takes a breath of air and his eyes become clear enough to register the beauty of the lake, a gift to him from the One who gives gifts to us all.

"And as he remembers all his pain, a great flock of black, quacking ducks lands on the lake, disturbing its smooth surface.

"One by one, he thinks of his daughters and wife; and each time he does, another great flock of ducks lands on the lake until there is no longer any room for the ducks to land on the surface, so the ducks must land on the ducks already there, pushing the first layer of ducks under the water, causing great noise with splashing and squawking. It is a symbol—the ducks are the pain that he is feeling, layered deep within him.

"As he sits by the lake grieving, more ducks come and more are forced under the water until the lake becomes a great, horrible black scene of suffering.

"Ayonwentha raises his eyes to heaven and from a deep place he asks the Great Spirit how a man can free himself from this kind of grief. And this is what happens:

"Ayonwentha realizes that the tears he has not shed have made him blind. When he learns he must 'wipe the tears from the grieving one's eyes,' he begins to cry and rivers of tears, great rapids of tears, rushing like a storm run down his face to the ground, to the lake. And a flock of ducks takes flight, and there is less noise and suffering.

"Then he realizes that he must brush the 'dust of death from his ears,' for anyone who grieves cannot hear what is clearly said. He suddenly hears the horror of the sound from the lake and he lets go of some deep part of grief. Simultaneously, a flock of ducks rises up from the water and now he can see a small bit of shining lake.

"He knows the medicine water of the lake can restore him. So he drinks from the lake and a wave of ducks rises once again out of the depths of the water. He lets go of some deep part of grief and many more ducks rise up into the sky, darkening the sun for a moment so that Ayonwentha is deeply afraid. In front of him Ayonwentha sees a beautiful, vast shimmering lake.

"He sits before the lake for a long time, his eyes clear, his ears clear, his heart clear. And he begins to sing in a voice that is clear from the healing power of the water. He thanks the Great Spirit for letting him see and hear and speak clearly once again. As the last ducks disappear, there is no trace of the shimmering lake. The ducks have taken it with them.

"Ayonwentha knows that his destiny is to return to his people and share what he has learned; and he travels back toward the land of the setting sun."

Katie and I understand at once why this story has resonated so strongly with Meb. She has been silently grieving for years. Maybe everything she has done has been in an effort to find peace. After hearing her tell this story, I give her a picture my father-in-law took at a lake in New Mexico where sand cranes cover the lake every evening and take flight each day with the first rays of sunlight.

"Those aren't ducks, you know," Meb jokingly pointed out.

"You get the message," I kidded her back, as we hung the framed picture over her bathroom sink, where she could see it everyday.

In Native American cultures, traditional stories are used to pass on life lessons that connect the people, nature, and their system of belief. Their stories express the concept of the supernatural along with the meaning of supernatural power. Their view of the world as a place alive with miracles breeds an intense awareness of the miraculous nature of life itself. The spiritual realm is intrinsic to—not isolated from—ordinary daily life. Eric Vormanns, our shaman, knew this and had tried to help us understand that the miraculous and supernatural are entwined as fundamental principles. He would have agreed that what we call miracles are a way for the "Great Spirit" to right a direction that has taken a wrong turn. The utter simplicity in connecting body, mind, and spirit reassured me and appealed to my faith in a benevolent Almighty.

Spiritual emphasis among Native Americans is on the earth and creation, where the earth and all it contains are cherished as family members. Watching Meb tend her garden as attentively and gently as though it were one of her children, I understood how this could be true. At one point in the past, we had had a parish priest who was Native American. He explained that in his culture what was important was handed down from generation to generation in the oral tradition. He never merely read the Gospel story—he recited it from memory, signaling its significance. While I knew many of these stories from hearing them repeated over the years, listening to him made them so much more meaningful than any of the Gospel readers I have heard either before or since.

As Catholics, the three of us had been steeped in miracle lore from a young age. Stories from the Old and New Testaments nourished our imaginations and became inseparable from the religious beliefs handed down from our parents. So too, the midrash of the Hebrew tradition, the hadith of the Islamic, the Jataka Tales of Buddha, and the adventures of Krishna—each reflects the central focus of stories within their belief systems. Like something out of *Ripley's Believe It Or Not,* many of the prophets and holy men within each of these faith traditions could heal, multiply, or punish their enemies with otherworldly power, all by calling upon God as they perceived him.

Miracles were not only a common experience—they played a leading role, containing common themes from the divine revelation of the holy books, as well as the prophetic and mystical qualities of the holy ones at the heart of their respective faiths. Turns out miracles were universally important as a sign of the Almighty's presence and support, not as the specific events in and of themselves. The one true God seems to be a veritable chameleon, changing colors not to blend in, but to stand out—calling others to faith.

As Katie tried to grasp the Native American concept of miracle, I told her about an experience Meb and I had shared a couple of years earlier. "I wish you had been there," I told her, "because the whole thing gave us new insights into ancient cultures.

"It was a warm California evening in March, and we decided on an impromptu barbeque, glad to be outside again," I began.

"I asked Bob and Gene and the kids if they knew that the Hale-Bopp comet was going overhead that night and told them that we were supposed to be able to see it. I was really excited. 'It only happens every zillion years and,' as extra enticement, I added 'it's also a lunar eclipse.' Meb was excited too, and followed me outside to look, but once out in the yard we realized the ambient neighborhood light limited our view.

"'No problem,' Meb told us and herded anyone who wanted to go into her van. She thought we should go to the park at the end of the canyon because it was really dark out there. We parked the van next to the picnic tables, but Gene and Bob insisted we hike up to the top of the nearby hill to be able see even more clearly. With the husbands in the lead, Meb and I took a bit more time. Actually, I was looking down, watching my step for rocks and snakes—the view from the picnic tables would have been just fine with me.

"When we got to the top of the hill and looked up, we were in the midst of a lunar eclipse, with the Hale-Bopp comet streaking overhead, and the stars in the heavens burning brightly. Magnificent. As we took in the enormity of the scene, we realized one of the 'stars' was moving, and quickly.

"Katie, you are not going to believe this. Gene told us that it wasn't a satellite—the trajectory was wrong. 'Oh my god,' I said as I realized it was the astronauts in the space station. The newspaper had said we might be able to see it as the sun reflects off the protective covering of the space station."

Meb cut short my reverie. "Can you just imagine what those in ancient cultures would have thought, experiencing this scene?"

"I'm sure virgins would have been sacrificed," I half-joked, glad those days were over.

"They were probably convinced that the end was near and would have done anything to be saved," Katie added.

Meb and I enjoyed reminiscing about the evening with Katie. Just as I was about to continue, ready to convince Katie that we had to include miracles from other cultures as a necessary part of our Chase, she beat me to it.

"We need to include other cultures like Native American in our miracle spectrum. I love the connection they have always made between nature and the Great Spirit."

Meb and I were thrilled to know Katie would now look forward to all I was uncovering from my multi-religious miracle search.

As in Native American oral history, the early religions were spoken traditions. Having played the game of "operator" as a child, and listening to the changes in the final version, it's hard to believe that any part of these religions survived unscathed. Religious documents, written down years (and sometimes centuries) later, for a different audience, must have been manipulated by authors and scrutinized by editors. The censors of the day would have worked to justify what had been written, striving to delete what they perceived as not germane or subject to the current version of political correctness.

Editorial license is hardly a modern phenomenon. As new and struggling religions began, it was important to eliminate fractures and factions, and perhaps some "truth" was lost in the name of a unified front. We don't need to look any further than our own family histories to understand how these legends or embellishments might have arisen. Stories about crazy Aunt Eloise or the daring of Cousin Phil, repeated over the years at family gatherings—usually packaged with some important moral or warning—take on a life of their own. It was easy to believe that ulterior motives and hidden agendas played a part in what was handed down in the religious family as well.

Surviving stories from a host of religious traditions provided insights into the truths, views, and ideas that formed them. This meant I was no longer tethered to the Council of Nicaea's opinion of what the "real" Christian stories were when it decided in the fourth century what should be included in the New Testament. The Gnostic gospels, unearthed in 1945 and dating back to the second century, were far more exciting. Full of adventures about the apostolic journeys, I laughed out loud when I read the purported letters between Jesus and the King of Edessa. In a letter to Jesus, complete with flattery and with an invitation to live out His years as an esteemed member of his court, the practical-minded king subtly sought a cure for his own ailment—besides, who wouldn't want a miracle worker at his beck and call? Apparently, the king's information-gathering system (i.e., network of spies) was quite good, because not only had he heard about Jesus' ability to heal the sick, he also knew about the political trouble that was brewing as a result of His miracle-working. The return note from Jesus declines the King's generous invitation, indicating that He has other plans that can't be put off or given to someone else, but promising to send His disciples to help. Clearly, Mary had taught her son to respond to correspondence in a timely and courteous manner!

In Eastern traditions, the message revealed through a story is every bit as important as the facts. Both Hinduism and Buddhism arose from ancient poems called the Vedas (2000 B.C.E.). Literally translated as knowledge, the Vedas reflected the role of miracles in two opposing views of the world. The first recognizes the world as a manifestation of the Absolute (in other words, God made us in His image and likeness—Baltimore Catechism 101). We look to God—the Absolute— as the keeper of the kingdom, who occasionally has to work miracles to maintain order. The other perspective identifies the world as an illusion. Miracles become feats of magic, easy to perform and manifest in this liberated state of being, en route to a state of nirvana.

Since Meb had told us that one of Bob's favorite books was the *Bhagavad Gita*, I thought it might be worthwhile to check it out, both from the standpoint of investigating Hindu thought, and also hoping it would shed some light on the ambivalent character I sensed in Bob at the same time. With the Hindu gods, miracles happen all the time because all that is, is of god. The god Vishnu enters the world at times of peril to preserve order, using Rama and Krishna as his human stand-ins. Both Rama and Krishna frequently perform miraculous feats to inspire love and devotion, to facilitate a state of bliss, or to show the ultimate nature of reality. In Krishna's view, all life is a manifestation of divine play, as he clones himself repeatedly and heads into the dell to enjoy as many maidens as possible. It's the first time I think to myself that maybe things don't bode well for Meb. Divine play is one thing, and though she tries hard to hide it, Bob's predilection for his own kind of play is beginning to show itself. With a healthy dose of wanderlust and disregard of the usual rules, Krishna routinely uses time and space travel to his advantage. I joked with Katie that perhaps Krishna had been reincarnated as Einstein, or at least must have been one of his early mentors.

Following on Krishna's heels, Siddhartha's transition from worldly prince to the transcendental Buddha established a new religion seeking to cultivate awakening. With the acknowledgement of the transience of the physical world and the goal of achieving perfection, Buddha, being self-enlightened, had no intrinsic need of performing miracles. Yet, in the interest of gaining followers, upon occasion even he succumbed to the pressure of the miracle "hard sell." In one tale, he entered the burrow of a serpent and emerged the next morning unscathed, engaging a new group of believers who went off throughout India proselytizing the tenets of Buddhism.

"Embedded in these Eastern religions are mystics, possessing extraordinary powers en route to seventh heaven," I announced at another miracle meeting. "Did you know that both Hindu and Buddhist saints have powers beyond the usual? They can see their previous lives and speak to animals—some can even fly!"

"Yeah, right," Katie responded. I didn't blame her. I had a hard time with this stuff myself.

"There are even examples of women who have miracle repertoires as good as, or better than, the men's." I knew at least she'd like that.

This discussion was right up Meb's alley, and I could tell she was excited that I had broached the subject first.

"Actually, in my research of female mystics, that fact is well known. Women have more visions, more ecstasies, more stigmata—all of it. They are also way more creative," she said. "Take St. Dorothy, who was pretty original with her miracle works. After being mocked and criticized for refusing to give up her faith, a suitor laughingly suggested she send him gifts from heaven. An angel supposedly appeared with the gifts, and Dorothy had the bouquet of flowers and apples from the Garden of Paradise delivered to him."

"Wait a minute, are you kidding me, Meb? You mean like an angelic FTD?" I exclaimed.

"That's exactly what I mean," said Meb. "And it worked. She lost her head but the guy was converted and all mocking ceased."

Actually, each time I read about the life of the saints, or Buddha, or any of the heroes of the world's religions, I found a tale more fantastic than the one before. I knew that the line between allegory and reality had been crossed, and yet, people became believers and would leave all they had known for the freedom of a new vision.

Buddha's admonition that a public miracle must be performed only with the intent to convert others to a higher ideal was consistent with what we found out about Muhammad, who chided his own idolaters centuries later:

God has not sent me to work wonders: He has sent me to preach to you. If signs be sought, let them be not of Muhammad's greatness, but of God's and for these one needs only to open one's eyes. The heavenly bodies holding their swift, silent course in the vault of heaven, the incredible order of the universe, the rain that falls to relieve a parched earth, palms bending with golden fruit, ships that glide across

the seas laden with goodness—can these be the handiwork
of gods of stone? What fools to cry for signs when creation
tokens nothing else?

I knew I had heard this message before! Cardinal Newman's sense of
creation as being only one of the thousands of miracles performed by
God was not so different from the Native American view, in which the
miracle of creation is an intrinsic and ongoing part of daily living.

In Islam, the Koran (Qur'an) or recitation is called "God's
standing miracle." During his own night of fire on the seventeenth
night of Ramadan (610 C.E.), Muhammad wrestled with the Angel
Gabriel on Mt. Hira for the first time, and, over the course of the
next twenty-three years, the words of the Koran were revealed to him.
While Muhammad was not a learned man, the exquisite beauty of the
language converted Arabs on the spot and was known to have come
directly from God. It has been said that Allah's words literally assaulted
Muhammad, as if they were solid and heavy. I enjoyed the graphic
legend, in which, during one of these transfixions, Muhammad was
riding on a camel, and by the time the revelation had ceased, though
the animal sought vainly to support the added weight of Allah's words,
its belly was pressed against the earth and its legs were splayed.

While hardly brazen about working miracles, Muhammad
is reputed to have performed his share, including the big three:
causing water to flow, food to multiply, and injuries to be healed.
Like other miracle workers, Muhammad's miracles were seen as a
means to an end—the conversion of new believers—and not the end
itself. His momentous escape from Mecca to Medina seems no less
remarkable than the exodus of the Jews from Egypt. On a night on
which he was certain to be killed, Muhammad hid in a cave, where
in a fast-forward version of nature, spiders and pigeons put up webs
and nests so that his pursuers, who were hot on his heels, passed by,
thinking the cave was deserted.

And yet not even Stephen King could have written a tale any
better than the hidden Imam and his possession of the Amanat or

sacred relics of Muhammad, including his cloak. This story has all the excitement of the escapades of other cloaked heroes: Superman, Batman, and Zorro, whose superhuman feats of daring include saving the world from evil by freeing the underdog from tyranny and oppression. Each of these fictional characters underscores the importance of Muhammad's cloak, worn by the leader of the Afghan Taliban, Omar, as proof of his position in Islam, as rightful ruler of the universe—the one who can intercede with God on man's behalf. Much as King Arthur of Camelot fame was recognized as the rightful heir to the throne after pulling the infamous sword from the stone, the legacy of Omar as the rightful leader was based on his ability to wrest the cloak from its secret location. Initially, Omar's followers were enthralled by the thought that the intermediary between God and man, the one who would save the world from evil, had returned. There was a belief that Omar would return at the end of time and would manifest his dominion, bringing order and justice to the world, taking vengeance on the enemies of God. But God is not a magic show, and without God there are no miracles. The power of perceived miracles in the wrong hands soon became very clear. In the swath of destruction that followed, not only were thousand-year-old Buddhist monuments destroyed, so were the hearts and souls of those who believed. I wish Omar had read the Vedas, for he would have learned that "hatred does not cease by hatred at any time; hatred ceases by love, this is an old rule."

Throughout history, miracles have been a pawn for religious manipulation, with catastrophic results. Using miracles as a bargaining chip is a dangerous road, with the proclamation that "My god is bigger, better, and more powerful than your god." The Jews of the Old Testament tell the story of God working many miracles on their behalf, sometimes to the great destruction of others, certainly—walls never just come "tumbling down" without wreaking havoc. In a sort of "my way or the highway" version of God, the horrors of the Crusades, the Inquisition, and the infamous witch trials all were undertaken in the name of religious zealotry. Fundamentalists in nearly all religions love to seize miracle stories from their holy books as literal examples of their selective, vengeful, and unforgiving God.

This relationship between miracles and evil troubled me. As I thought about the miracles in our lives, it wasn't possible to ignore the evil or dark side of the events that occurred. Katie described with great visceral detail the transformation of her would-be assailant as he became full of evil and ready to pounce; and had evil not flooded the nanny as Elizabeth was so brutally shaken, the miracles that propelled us forward would hardly have been necessary. While in early times the supernatural was an accepted part of life, there was an acknowledgement that its power could be used for either good or evil.

While I had never doubted that miracles were good, I too had seen the face of Evil over the many months I faced cancer and hoped for a cure. At one of our phone meetings, I had explained to Katie and Meb that I had felt Evil's presence while alone with my thoughts. It was an absence of hope, as the temptation to despair loomed in front of me. I understood Evil's need to feed itself on all that is good, waiting patiently for our humanness to fail and our precious positive energy to dissipate. Evil has no power of its own and exists only from the power we give it. Like nature abhorring a vacuum, once we are empty, Evil steps in to fill the void, and its face becomes our own. Katie reminded me that I had good reason to go on living joyfully—I knew I was lucky—but I had to keep reminding myself of that fact. In the process, I became more understanding of those who had given up and turned their lives over to despair— those who had lost all hope, and in the process, lost themselves. In despair, we give up and lose control of our emotions, becoming raw, unfeeling spirits of the flesh.

Meb understood how I had worried a lot about Evil as a child. Educated by the Irish nuns in Boston, I saw Evil in their descriptions of James Joyce and Frank O'Connor. She remembered those stories as well from school and from her Irish aunt, the nun. We laughed about how I had been scared out of my wits by a story about the devil appearing as a normal person, except for the scorched bedposts he left in his wake. I explained to Meb, the real problem was that it was about this same time that my teacher told us that any of us could actually be little devils in disguise. I had lived in dread. After a long period of internal debate and scary nightmares, and contrary to the opinions of my siblings, I decided that while I was certainly no angel, I wasn't a devil either, disguised or otherwise. It was a huge relief.

On a night I will always remember in the middle of my cancer treatment, when I was sicker than ever, and alone, since everyone else in the house was asleep, I felt doomed, ready to give up and succumb to Evil's spell. It became my personal Night of Fire. I was afraid, but somehow I found the strength to pray. Within moments, Gene was by my side. I felt the positive energy of God in my husband's rescue, protecting me from the despair that threatened to take over my spirit. With God's continuing grace, I hope to never be in the position of giving in to Evil's malevolent claim.

Like Muhammad and so many others, I have come to realize that the importance of miracles is in the realm of what happens next, not in the here and now. I love feeling connected with other religions, and, as Katie would say, I've begun to feel more comfortable in my skin, recognizing that by choosing one way to live, I've made a positive choice that will bring me closer to the Almighty, not farther away from those who make different choices. "We may climb the mountain from different paths, but the view from the summit is identical for all. . . ." Six Degrees of Separation has become my way to look at the universe, not just a movie.

10

NOT AFRAID OF THE DARK

Above all, faith is the opening of an inward eye, the eye of the heart,
to be filled with the presence of Divine light.

—THOMAS MERTON, NEW SEEDS OF CONTEMPLATION

MEB

Joan's right: to look into the face of Evil takes courage. It takes courage to see that darkness is a part of each one of us. Katie's recurrent dream after her father's death taught her that. To be a saint must require the ability to see the dark potential, be willing to name it, and choose light instead, like Augustine at his breaking point and his serendipitous choice of readings. I have come to believe that living in light is a choice; I acknowledge darkness, but choose to focus elsewhere.

I heard a story once about a three-year-old who went into a diabetic heart attack. The doctors put a needle directly into her heart to start it back up again. When this little one regained consciousness, she told the pediatrician she had seen herself lying on the bed and three doctors had come into the room to take her someplace else. "How did you know they were doctors?" he asked. "Well, they all wore white and they had bright lights in their bodies!" she exclaimed. These "brightly lit doctors" had told her that she could push the red button and go with them, or the green button and stay with her mother. She picked the green one.

I think my infant daughter saw this light. I think she was given a choice to go with the light or return into my arms. Now my daughter is a beautiful young woman, and she is still drawn to the ephemeral light. Many white-coated doctors have told us, "She sees nothing and has no light perception." We know they are wrong. Not only does Liz see light, but light shines from inside of her like a beacon to the countless number of people she touches with her indomitable spirit. Light from within her mind's eye lights up her life.

My experiences with Elizabeth and others have taught me that witnesses, as well as victims, can be affected by their traumatic experiences. It is difficult to remain clear-headed, to be calm, and to see more than fragments of the whole picture. A natural defense mechanism is built into our minds and hearts for survival, breaking the experience into pieces so we don't get overwhelmed. We retain "sound bites," bits of images, smells, feelings, words, jumbled up in time and fragmented, making it difficult to make sense of the enormity of any atrocity.

This is why I tell Joan and Katie that our memories may not be completely accurate. The flood of emotions present during times of high stress, pain, or fear influence our vision and the accuracy of our recollections. Eyewitnesses are often unable to recall important details or may even make up details that are not there. I am not surprised when each one of us Miracle Chasers has a slightly different take on the same experience. In spite of how my rational mind is frustrated by my inability to sequence and recall clear details, I tell them that we must be witnesses: each one of us has a miracle story to tell and a destiny that only we can bring to life.

Like Joan and Katie, I too feel that I have looked into the face of Evil and survived. Unlike Joan and Katie, my version is not a life-or-death confrontation. Early on in my days as a child advocate, I was frequently asked to speak to the media about the legislation I was working on and how parents could protect themselves and their child from abuse in childcare. It was so grueling that sometimes I would try to negotiate with God so I would not have to leave home. I knew it was my calling to "bear witness" to my story as a way to move legislation along in order to protect children or to provide funds for quality childcare, but my life was complicated and the emotional expense was high. I used to say "Do I have to go, God? Please, can't someone else do this?" Sometimes the producer of a television program or radio show would let me do a remote live spot. Sometimes I could find another parent to take my place. And sometimes the show had *my* name on it and I *had* to be the one to go.

When I was seven months pregnant with my youngest child, Daniel, I was flown to Chicago overnight to be on a national talk show. The trip was exhausting. It was a very hot July, and I was very pregnant. I went with the clear intention of telling our family's story in a way as to empower people, parents, and child advocates to work together and end maltreatment in childcare. Once there, I met other parents with terrible tragedies to share. I wanted to be able to point the audience toward something specific they could do to stop child abuse. Our stories had to be given meaning. We all have to choose how to respond to the horrible events a few courageous parents shared on national television. But it didn't happen that way. My vision—that together we would put sorrow into words and then into action— seemed to become just one more sob story trading shock value for ratings.

On the way home, I felt defeated and completely spent. As I was looking mindlessly out the window of the plane, flying high above at thirty thousand feet, I suddenly had such an intense visceral sensation that the hair on my skin prickled in goose bumps. Though there was nothing but clouds and sky outside the window, I felt a presence, as if I were looking straight into the face of Evil. At that moment, I absolutely knew that in order to spread evil in the world, one would need to look no further than attacking the Child—the lightness in every being, so evident in the young and helpless. "For, such as these is the Kingdom made." Create anger, despair, and the loss of imagination by wounding the potential of the Child, and the world suddenly is looking into the Abyss.

Evil looks like giving up—giving up trying to protect not only children, but that most sacred part of ourselves, the dancing light within us. Evil lurks in watching me or another mother emote on television and then turning away, convinced that "It won't ever happen to me because . . ." When we make decisions to protect our shallow sense of safety, building on the belief that if we do everything right, nothing bad will ever happen to us, Evil has a chance. One of the reasons I think people don't talk about miracles is because they are afraid that by doing so, attention will be drawn to a sad, or desperate, or lonely, or fragile part of themselves that they don't want to admit to, much less share with others. You have to admit that you are in the foxhole in order to be saved. Ignoring Evil promotes our autonomy at the expense of our connection to each other. If we think that the bad things that happen to other people will never happen to us, because we didn't do that Thing they did (meet Ted Bundy, hire a neighbor's nanny for a few hours, get sick), why do we need to fight for change, step up to be involved in the world around us, make a difference? Why believe in miracles? Why are miracles even necessary?

Once home, I tell my family a little bit about the intense experience I had on the plane. Andrew, now four, and Bob look baffled. They ask me to pass the potatoes, pretty much wanting things to get back to normal. But six-year-old Elizabeth solemnly says, "Mommy, we can't let the bad guys win. I'm going to help you." I hug her for a moment, kiss her head, and feel a kindred spirit.

Years later, as I help Elizabeth pack for college, I think about how our experiences have helped her get ready for this point. All the people who made choices to step up for her: Fran, Liz's Braille teacher, our personal Annie Sullivan; the teachers of the visually impaired; Guide Dogs for the Blind and the puppy raisers who raised and trained Bonds, her first guide dog, to name a few. I think about how Liz was as a baby, toddler, and child. Stubborn. Determined. Assertive. Demanding. What an imagination! What a Spirit! It was a balancing act—a village supported her soul. I am sometimes overwhelmed, just thinking about the journey.

How many children have been saved by the legislation that followed Liz's abuse? How many professionals were inspired by her small, still voice speaking clearly and passionately about standing up for children and children's rights; the songs and poetry about shaken angels that educated families and legislators about Shaken Baby Syndrome? My proud mama-heart hears a phrase from Isaiah as if he were talking about my daughter too: "And a little child shall lead them."

The child who inspired teachers, lawmakers, and child advocates by her very presence has now become a wonderful, intelligent, illuminating soul who truly believes and has personally experienced how one person can make a difference. In short, I think she is A Miracle. She desperately wants to lead a normal life. Like her mama, she knows how to work hard and pray hard for help in trying to achieve her dreams.

It's the summer before Liz's freshman year in college. She and I have driven down to Stanford many times to spend long, hot hours walking the campus with a guide dog trainer so that both Liz and Bonds will be able to manage the large, sprawling university. When school begins, Liz wants to "just be a student." It's complicated; Liz needs to get a course schedule and dorm assignment early so that she can learn her routes in advance. After several frustrating false starts through the proper channels, she is getting nowhere and takes matters into her own hands. Using the voice reader on her computer to look up names of the housing staff, she finds a responsive individual. Like an immigrant in a strange, new land, Liz finally connects with a friendly stranger who takes her in and opens the first door. This one kind person leads to another, and then another, until at last, a meeting is set up with someone who may be able to help. The meeting is scheduled for a few weeks later, on a Tuesday evening at 5:00 P.M.—not the most convenient time to head through San Francisco during rush hour, but it's the only time the person can meet with Liz about her guide dog and what she needs. Liz is anxious to go, prepared and determined to take charge of her life. At eighteen, this can be expected. I celebrate her independence and how she made this happen.

Except, the meeting is scheduled for 5:00 in the afternoon of Tuesday, September 11, 2001.

Liz calls to reschedule, but they tell us it's now or never. The decision to go is hers.

On this day, the country reels, horrified by the terrorist attacks on the World Trade Center and the Pentagon. The freeway, usually packed with cars trying to fit through the tiny tunnel that connects one side of the East Bay hills with the other, is eerily empty. As we cross the Bay Bridge, a possible "target" in my mind, my tires click against the bumps in the road in tempo with the jarring nature of my thoughts. I keep thinking this could be my last moment, and my last moment, and my last, until we are on the other side. The threat of additional attacks is palpable in every radio commentator's voice, and I listen for any warning as I pretend to check the Traffic Report. Liz stays focused; she does not want to be late.

I realize how terrified I am when I notice that I am cold beyond imagining on this hot late-summer day. My hands are shaking, and I grip the steering wheel so hard that there are indentations of my nails in my palms. A slight buzzing in my head, like the beginning of a memory I want to forget, begins. I realize I've felt this way before, in the hospital room, waiting to hear if Liz will survive the night, wondering what will become of my six-month-old infant who a neighbor's nanny has just tried to murder.

I turn to Liz, who asks if we can play her new country-western CD. I am grateful to turn off the news. I long for reassurance and realize that the Angel of Mass Media will not protect me. The simple songs belt out Americana. I exhale.

I tell Liz: "Today makes me remember how much evil is in the world. I feel like I did when you were abused. That's when I first realized how dark and terrible human beings can be to one another; when I really understood that evil is real, is present, and that it touches me when it touches others." I seem to be rambling. I want so badly to connect with her.

Liz slowly faces me and turns down the volume. She smiles and says simply, "Today I feel so grateful to be alive, Mom." We talk more. We are both so affected by the violence and the terror. It takes all of my courage to keep driving Liz to her meeting, her destiny, but I do.

Liz's ability to feel grateful for life is one of her gifts to me and to the world. Again and again, I am stunned by the way my daughter, the survivor, looks at living. I want her faith, her joy in the moment, and her courage. I want to warm up to the world and feel blessed, even as I face evil and death.

I park the car in a nearby lot and walk with her and her guide dog to the residence-hall door, holding it open. She grabs Bonds's leather harness and walks in for the meeting, saying, "See you soon."

I find a bench outside on the patio and sit down amid the manicured flowers. The only sound is a tinkling fountain in the middle of the empty courtyard. It is intensely quiet, as if even the birds are afraid to take to the skies. "It's time to let her go," I say, "no matter how dangerous the world is."

In this residence-hall courtyard, I say good-bye to my baby. As Army planes and helicopters fly overhead, I wait for my young adult daughter, My Miracle, to emerge, full of promise and full of hope.

11

CLIMB EVERY MOUNTAIN

Let us therefore approach the throne of grace with boldness,
so that we may receive mercy and find grace to help in time of need.

—HEBREWS 4:14–16

JOAN

While Meb was packing and carrying physical baggage getting Liz ensconced at Stanford, I found myself recognizing that a diagnosis of cancer brings with it a lot of emotional baggage. First is the fear—some even say that's the worst part. The not-knowing: how bad is it, how much time do I have, will it be painful, what will happen to the people I love? It's like watching your world go by in fast forward with all of its highs and lows, kind of like when you stick your hand out the car window while driving seventy miles an hour and the slightest movement sends your arm flailing in different directions.

Once I got past my initial inertia, lying on the couch and feeling sorry for myself, life was busy as I got past two more surgeries and finished with my six months of chemotherapy. It was only with all of that behind me that I began the road to recovery. By the way, the road to recovery actually sounds a lot easier than it is in real life. I had no hair, I'd gained more weight than I ever had in my whole life (including three pregnancies)—and, to add insult to injury, I had also experienced significant word loss from chemo-brain. It was really tough to be writing a book when I couldn't complete a sentence, much less a whole paragraph. The physicians also kept me on a very short leash.

Every three months, I was back at the dreaded doctor's office for more tests and checkups. It's really hard to think that you are normal or healthy when you feel like there is a cancer hospital with your name on it. Bottom line is, you want to believe you are well—cured, even: that you have beaten the odds. You hope the cancer is under control, but you still have to live with the constant reminder that it could come back. After the tragedy of 9/11, I frequently thought that everyone in the U.S. now knew what it's like to have a cancer diagnosis. One day you feel great, and the next you have been dealt a blow so horrific and central to your well-being that all semblance of control is shattered. It's like being in limbo, constantly waiting for the other shoe to drop; waiting to be squashed without warning, thinking you are safe and suddenly it's a death sentence.

This was how I was feeling when I read a holiday article about Artie Boyle, cancer survivor and miracle man. The article first caught my eye as a human-interest story, and the name of his friend was the name of a friend of mine, but the world was not that small and I didn't know his friend. Yet there was something compelling about his story; and, after all, we were looking for current miracle stories in addition to those in historical records. Artie had been diagnosed with renal cell cancer that had spread to his lung. I knew enough to know that this was not good. The father of thirteen (a miracle in itself, as far as I was concerned), Artie was quite a guy. Yes, he had a killer cancer diagnosis, but he wasn't dead yet, and his golfing buddies persuaded him to go to a Marian shrine in Yugoslavia. Medjugorje (med-jew-gor-yay) was a place that, no matter how hard I tried, I could never pronounce properly; and though I wanted to know more about the things that happened there, I just hadn't gotten around to it. While he was there, Artie claimed to have experienced a miracle: the cancer in his chest evaporated. Poof.

Artie called his wife and asked her to schedule another MRI and to cancel the surgery to remove his lung. His doctor was not happy. In fact, he fired him—that is, the physician fired the patient. So Artie found another physician at the same hospital. This physician had come to believe in the existence of a spiritual nuance, one he couldn't medically explain, through his experience with his own aged parents as they faced the end of their lives. He agreed to re-scan Artie. This time there was no more big spot on his lung. No big spot meant no cancer, and no cancer meant no surgery. Needless to say, Christmas for the Boyle family that year was pretty wonderful.

Great, I thought: the other shoe didn't drop. Yet. I was still pretty skeptical. In fact, I surely wasn't ready to call it a miracle, though the newspaper did. For several years, I kept the article on my desk among the myriad miracle stories I had resolved to pursue one day. As it turned out, as I retreated from my cancer therapy, so did Artie, and as I went on to live, so did he. Perhaps I was beginning to feel more confident. Maybe you could really beat this thing, or perhaps I was more ready to believe in what had happened to him. I mean, if he could still be alive when by all rights he should be dead, then it could certainly be a good sign for me. I decided that maybe it was a miracle after all.

Four years later, an article in the paper about Artie's son mentioned Artie's miracle and identified the location of their home, which was just south of Boston. By now, Katie's daughter Laura was in college at Harvard, and Katie became a regular visitor to the East Coast, especially during the volleyball season. I thought it was time for the two of us to take another field trip. Not to Marin County this time, but to Hingham, Massachusetts, and trust me, not much that happens in Hingham could be classified as bizarre. In fact, it would be hard to find a place more commonplace—hardly an exotic address for a real miracle.

Besides the obvious human-interest story, we were intrigued with Artie's connection to another miraculous place so similar to Lourdes and Fatima. I called directory assistance, got Artie's number, and gave him a call. As Katie would say, it was as simple as that. He agreed to meet with us, but mentioned it would have to be after the *Good Morning America* interview he had done, scheduled to air as part of their miracle series on Friday mornings. I thought he had to be kidding. Since when did miracles become a *Good Morning America* mainstream topic, not to mention important enough to merit a whole series, with the tagline of "Miracle Fridays"? And when did my guy, Artie, the guy I had been watching for the last four years—truth be told, waiting for him to die and at the same time dreading his death—make it to the big time?

We met in Artie's office, and, unlike Eric the shaman's, there was no exotic wall art, just pictures of family and friends and a couple of action hockey shots featuring Artie's son, currently on the team at Boston College, my alma mater and the reason I had been drawn to the sports article in the first place. Artie put us at ease right away with a ready smile, firm handshake, and warm welcome. "So, what's up?" he asked. We gave him the quick version of our book and asked him to describe his experience.

I had to laugh. Did you ever feel like a third wheel? Well, that would be me, because Artie only had eyes for Katie. On the ride down, Katie and I had decided that she would be the "question person," because while I had researched the Medjugorje shrine and was a "Mary person" all along, it was Katie who was trying so hard to be all logical and scientific. I had watched the *Good Morning America* piece, and I already believed the miracle in Artie's story—I just wanted more specifics. But Katie was yet to be convinced. She posed her questions. What happened? What did you feel like? Has this experience changed your life? It seemed as if Katie's list was endless, but Artie was patient, his demeanor never reflecting frustration with her continuous line of questioning. Artie described his experience, the importance of forgiveness, of prayer, the closeness of Mary to Medjugorje. He described his final letting go, the release of his anger, his angst, his laid-bare openness to the hand of God. I guess he was describing his faith. Not Sunday-school faith, but his reach-into-your-gut-and-pull-it-out, tears-in-the-eyes, knock-'em-down-drag-'em-out faith. He became acutely aware of an intense moment of release. A sense of peace enveloped him and he was no longer afraid. At the same time, there was something else. Deep down in his chest, he felt it. A something, a who-knows-what, a certainty that whatever bad that was in there, wasn't bad any more. It was an eerie description, this chest thump atop a remote mountain in Yugoslavia. But happily, the proof was in the pudding, which in this case was an MRI. Although medical science said Artie should have been dead already, he sure looked pretty healthy to us. After meeting him and hearing his story, I realized his miracle was safe with me.

But for Katie, it was even more—she recounted the tortuous path of Mary in her own life. She asked, maybe naïvely, maybe in earnest, "Why all these trails, why me, why Mary?" By now, you may have noticed that Katie really likes to ask questions. That's when Artie looked Katie straight in the eye and held her gaze as if I didn't even exist in the room. His answer left Katie speechless: "She's calling you. No. Not Joan, not Meb. *You*, she wants you to believe and to understand. No one *goes* to Mary; you have to be called."

Katie doesn't recall the tears in her eyes, but I do.

Okay, so first Ted Bundy doesn't kill you, and then Mary—as in Mary the Mother of God—calls you. What's a girl like Katie to do?

Like the day we visited Eric, Katie and I felt that with Artie as well, we had been in the presence of a real-life, down-to-earth person who got it; someone who understood a big part of the Big Picture that we had been trying to bring into focus.

Our meeting with Artie provided the framework for our next miracle meeting and centered our discussion on some of the shrines and holy places where miracles occur. I thought it was a good opportunity to suggest that Katie and Meb make some time to watch *The Song of Bernadette* movie, which Katie had found on one of her excursions to Berkeley.

Not long after Katie's return to California after our meeting with Artie, she and Meb, armed with popcorn and comfy chairs, did just that. While Meb likes movies because they serve as a good distraction from an already distracting life, Katie is a movie maven and critic. She watches them, she re-watches them; she remembers lines and characters and can replay whole scenes from start to finish. It must have something to do with the years she spent starring in high-school musicals. Being a great movie critic is one of her many talents. Katie called me after she and Meb had watched the movie, and frankly that's when I knew for sure that Katie had just been humoring me all along when she said "Wow, that was a really good movie." Now, mind you, it had won the Academy Award for Best Picture, and the new actress Jennifer Jones, who played the part of Bernadette, won the Oscar for Best Actress; but for Katie, seeing is believing, and *The Song of Bernadette* now had her Good House-keeping Seal of Approval.

This gave me the incentive I needed to open the thick book that was the basis for the movie, which Meb had given me as a gift one Christmas. As a child, I'd had a condensed picture-book version with a beautiful golden-colored cover that came with its own 45-RPM record, which at the time was very extravagant. When I finally opened the "real" book, I was enthralled just reading the author's note and realizing the story behind *The Song of Bernadette.* The author, Franz Werfel, told a miraculous tale of survival from his World War II experience in Nazi Germany. In Europe in the late 1930s, most famous Jews had already left their native countries, but Franz and his wife remained. They realized too late that they had stayed too long, even though it was well known that they were at the top of the Nazi hit list. After the Austrian Anschluss in 1938, they kept one step ahead of the enemy in an ongoing attempt to get over the Spanish border from France. Through a series of events, their exodus took them to Lourdes, where they stayed planning their perilous escape.

With his compatriots murdered, amid rumors of death camps, Franz must have been completely crazed, second-guessing and berating himself. Why hadn't they left earlier like everyone else? He should have known better. He was married to Alma Schindler, the widow of the famous composer Gustav Mahler, renowned as the most beautiful woman in Europe, and he had now jeopardized her life as well as his own. It was there and then, staring probable death in the face, that Lourdes got through to him. He watched pilgrims come and go to the grotto for physical as well as spiritual healing. After a while, he too made a daily pilgrimage to the grotto. Though he was a nonbeliever, he found himself recognizing that Lourdes was indeed a special place: a place of possibilities, even a place of miracles. He promised that if he escaped with his life, he would write the story of Lourdes. Finally, after five weeks, it was time to escape. Even though the *New York Post* had already reported his death, his group headed over the mountains. While not particularly ancient at age fifty, Franz was overweight and out of shape, and he had a heart condition as well as the effects of a prior heart attack, all of which kept him from overexerting himself. A trip on foot over sparsely traveled, rugged mountains was *not* what the doctor had ordered. But he didn't have a choice, and he was able to make the climb even faster than his companions, averting capture and death, finally reaching the relative safety of Spain and Portugal en route to the United States.

Werfel was good on his word and wrote the book in 1941, shortly after his arrival in southern California. Not only was he inspired, but his book resonated with others, and a movie was made the next year. Winning the Academy Award in 1943 with World War II still raging must have been surreal for this Jewish refugee, an acknowledgement of professional success in a new land based upon his belief in miracles. Tragically, only a short time later, his heart gave out; Franz died at age fifty-five, leaving *The Song of Bernadette* as a final testament.

Apparently, we hadn't yet shed the Death by Miracle theme we had discovered while researching the Enlightenment. While we now could joke about it, we nonetheless recognized that chasing miracles was not only intensely personal as we identified miracles that spoke to us individually; it was an emotional experience as well—you can't think of the salvation of a loved one without considering the flip side, the what-might-have-been. The "what-if," as Katie says. We felt that passion in our personal interaction with Artie, and in reading the words of Werfel, and we knew it was time to give voice to the pressing question at the center of our Chase: "What is a miracle?" But this time, instead of feeling intimidated or insecure, we felt buoyed by all we had learned and were beginning to understand.

Part Five

THE RIPPLE EFFECT

"Look out!" We cry, *"it's alive"* . . .
An "impersonal God"—well and good.
A subjective God of beauty, truth and goodness,
Inside our own heads—better still.
A formless life-force surging through us,
A vast power which we can tap—best of all.
But God Himself, alive, pulling at the
other end of the cord,
Perhaps approaching at an infinite speed . . .
That is quite another matter. . . .
Supposing we really found Him?
We never meant it to come to *that*!
Worst still, supposing He had found us?

C. S. LEWIS, *Miracles*

12

MIRACLE MIXERS

God is in the midst of the city.

—PSALM 46

KATIE

When Meb and I called Joan for our next meeting, I recapped our movie evening. I repeated a line from the movie that had stuck with me.

"'For those who believe [in miracles], no explanation is necessary; for those who do not believe, no explanation is possible.' You've been holding out on me, Joan; you could have saved me a lot of work if you had shared that sentiment with me a few years back," I teased her.

"I still can't believe Katie made us watch the part where they call out 'Luise' three times, so we could imagine your miracle moment together," Meb added. "As if I wasn't there with you and saw the whole thing unfold."

"You guys are hysterical," Joan exclaimed.

"I gotta say, it was pretty uncanny," I told them. "After the movie, I told Meb more about our visit with Artie."

"Sounds like Artie really got to her," Meb observed.

I felt like Joan and I had traded places during the meeting with Artie. "The proof is in the MRI," Joan said later. Since when does Joan need proof? And though I may have crossed the line just a tad in terms of being an impartial interviewer, I do not remember this conversation as two-sided, and I certainly don't remember Artie telling me that "you have to be called." Good grief. Joan insists I'm suffering from got-too-intense-for-me memory block. That said, I was uncharacteristically accepting of his story and didn't need to see the MRI to believe it to be true.

Artie Boyle was approachable, kind, and open to my questions. I saw him as a kindred spirit, someone who'd had an obvious divine encounter and could give me some perspective and answers. Turns out he was in a different league, a practicing Catholic in possession of great faith: faithful, as in full of faith. After I met him, I determined right away that my "kindred spirit" aspirations had been so much wishful thinking. I had made faith complicated, overthought it, maybe even sabotaged it. He embodied his faith, practiced it in a way that became who he was, no deliberation required. If anybody deserved a miracle, Artie did, with all those kids and all that faith. Whatever happened on the mountaintop, he forgot about his desperation for a physical cure, and the peace of mind and soul he felt were all that really mattered. Then he got the cure anyway. Meeting Artie made me feel my spiritual inadequacies, but he also gave me hope.

While I am a work in progress today, I was hardly a poster child for religion or spirituality back in the 1970s, when I experienced my own miracle, which makes me wonder—where do faith and miracles intersect? In the New Testament there is the story of the hemorrhaging woman (Luke 8:46) who, defying the customs of the time, touches Jesus' cloak in a crowd and is instantly healed. Jesus tells her: "My daughter, your faith has made you well. Go in peace." Faith and healing and peace seem to go together. There is also the story of Jesus' appearance to "Doubting Thomas" (John 20:27), when he commanded Thomas to "Stop your doubting and believe!" For Thomas, only his personal experience led to faith. Now there's my kind of kindred spirit! And Joan found this sentiment in George Bernard Shaw's play *Saint Joan*, spoken by the Archbishop: "A miracle, my friend, is an event that creates faith. They may seem very wonderful to the people who witness them, and very simple to those who perform them. That does not matter: if they confirm or create faith they are miracles." Besides wondering why Joan was reading *Saint Joan*—though I can take a wild guess—I do think the Archbishop was on to something.

Our meeting with Artie was one more clue, one more story that we hoped, when taken together with years of exploration and debate, would give us our answer to the *big* question: What is a miracle? I had felt particularly desperate to answer this question after an experience I had at a high-school Parents' Association gathering. As a liberal, independent college preparatory school near Berkeley, things like politics and religion are on their "Don't ask, don't tell" list. Our family was fairly new to the school at the time, so I made my way to the only person I knew, Rebecca, who was standing with two other women on an outside patio. She introduced me and announced that I was writing a book about miracles. Since I was certain this was going to be the conversation stopper of all time, I was stunned when all three erupted with enthusiasm.

"What an interesting idea!"

"Tell us, what have you found out?"

"Katie has quite a story herself," Rebecca threw in.

Finally, one of my new acquaintances wanted to know, "So, Katie, what exactly *is* a miracle?"

Fortunately for me, there was barely a pause in the conversation before one of the women shared a story about a cousin's near-death experience and the absolute certainty held by some in her family that it had indeed been a miracle (though she didn't agree). Then Rebecca mentioned a harrowing experience her daughter, Laura Beth, had lived through earlier that year as an exchange student in South America. On a kayak trip with her closest friend, just as the guide and her friend rounded a bend in the river, Laura Beth's kayak capsized. She struggled to right the kayak but was unable to turn it back over. Desperately she tried to release herself from the upside-down boat and couldn't get out. Panicked and within seconds of losing consciousness, her "life passed before her." Suddenly, a powerful force reached around her and flipped the kayak right-side up. Rebecca's daughter has no explanation for the experience, other than being certain it was the "hand of God."

Even though we did not share the same religious traditions, we were captivated by the telling of stories and what they might mean. For me, it meant I didn't have to answer the question "What exactly is a miracle?" At least, I didn't have to answer it that night. The question lingered, though. It's not that it wasn't floating around in my head before then; it just got noisier and more constant, like a radio station with static.

Meb, Joan, and I had wrestled with the question from the beginning, and with passion. I had what I called "minimum standards" for a miracle. Meb saw the subsequent events that unfolded after Elizabeth was abused as a miracle.

"Katie, even the miracle of Creation continues to unfold," she tried to explain to me.

We did agree on the obvious. Miracles could be big and influential, having consequences for the whole world; or they could be small and private, like the ones at the heart of this book. Beyond these basics, we continued to disagree over the definition in a way that was so emotionally charged, we had to let it go. No resolution. Meb called it the elephant in the room. Joan figured we'd work it out eventually.

This is what happens when three strong women attack a big question. As our Chase got under way, none of us was reluctant to weigh in with an opinion. We decided early on that we would have to check our egos at the door and agreed that the Miracle Chase was bigger than we were. Words and phrases like connectedness, open and trusting, effort, energy, and generosity of spirit had gone up on our flipchart at one of our early meetings. As the years passed, we became less judgmental and more aware. Now, years from the beginning of our journey, I became the one charged with answering the question. Ironic, since initially I'd had the narrowest vision. Translation: I was the most judgmental and the least aware. Meb and Joan had faith in more than God as they patiently encouraged my transformation from Miracle Gatekeeper to Miracle Spokeswoman. I was ready to open the guard gates wide.

The more stories we heard or read about, the more our own ideas changed and—at least in my case—expanded. It's hard to pick a favorite, but there is one story that was a breakthrough for me; it was open-ended and messy, as miracle stories go. The author, Ann Hood, tells of her personal devastation after her father is diagnosed with inoperable lung cancer. Obviously, I could relate to this part—but the rest of her story is inspiring in a way I could never have duplicated at the time my own father was dying. She decides to take a trip from her home on the East Coast to Chimayo, New Mexico, a small town near Santa Fe, where she has heard of a chapel containing red dirt said to result in miraculous cures. Before departing El Santuario de Chimayo with a zip-lock bag full of the precious dirt, she kneels and prays, "Please let my father's tumor go away."

Upon returning home, she learns her father has just been rushed to the hospital, critically ill with pneumonia and in respiratory failure. She immediately sets out for the hospital with her little baggie and asks her father to hold some of the dirt in his hand. Within twenty-four hours, he has a bizarre experience when he literally sees the tumor leave his body, "like sparks, agitated and angry." The next day, a scan proves what her father knew to be true: the tumor has disappeared. However, the pneumonia has weakened him to such an extent that he dies from complications a few months later. A year after her father's death, Ms. Hood returned to the chapel in Chimayo to offer thanks for her answered prayer and also to pray for "peace of mind" and "the courage to accept what had come my way." With the grace she possessed to return to Chimayo, I hope her prayer was answered.

Joan and Meb talk a lot about healing miracles, and how there is often a healing of the spirit inherent in the healing of the body. Even when a prayer doesn't bring the physical cure, peace of mind can still be found, a spiritual metamorphosis wrapped up in every prayer for help. Maybe when we are at our most vulnerable and desperate, we are also most open to hearing God. In Ms. Hood's story about the death of her father, she seems to have understood that prayer relates more to acceptance than to miracles; and yet we can all relate to the asking. What if praying was the one thing standing between you and a miracle? I think that's why they say there are no atheists in foxholes.

The Chimayo story made the "What is a miracle?" question more complicated. Ms. Hood got exactly what she asked for: her father's tumor did indeed go away; yet we all know that what she really wanted was for her father to become well. She won the battle but lost the war. The story forced me to look at the question differently, to peel back another layer. Kind of like the Matryoshka dolls from Russia, where inside each doll is a smaller doll, and all you know with each newly discovered doll is that you are one step closer to the final one. As the three of us searched to unwrap the layers covering the essence of "miracle," we agreed that the experience of Alexis Carrel, someone we had all come across in our chase, provided further illumination of a miracle's many layers: the external event we all think of, but also the deep and lasting soulful shift that can follow; how one person's experience unfolds.

In 1902, Alexis Carrel was a highly regarded French physician who, as a product of his time, had abandoned the Catholic faith for the rationalism of the scientific mind. Dr. Carrel was disturbed by reports of miraculous healings at the grotto in Lourdes, France. When he received an invitation to observe sick patients on one of the trains to Lourdes, he knew this was his opportunity to dispel the fervor associated with the place, to prove that Lourdes was make-believe. He examined many of the patients on the train before their arrival and was particularly interested in a young woman, Marie Bailly, who had indisputable evidence of fatal tuberculosis peritonitis. She was so near death that he was afraid she would not even make it to the end of the train journey, much less to the grotto itself. He was able to document her symptoms, which included obvious abdominal tumors. He was so sure that she, of all the patients he examined, could not possibly be cured that he told a colleague that, if it were to happen, "I would become a monk!" She was brought to the grotto, but, since she was too ill to be immersed, water from the pools was brought to her and sprinkled on her abdomen. As he watched her intently, she slowly began to wake up and become alert. Dr. Carrel began to notice a change in the color of her skin and the brightness in her eyes. He knew this had to be his mind playing tricks on him. He found the atmosphere to be overwhelming—the vast numbers of faithful lifted their collective voices in prayer, creating a deafening onslaught of sound and emotion. No wonder there was healing for those who suffered from what he rationalized were psychosomatic symptoms. As he continued to observe his patient, however, the unthinkable occurred. In front of his eyes, the sheet covering the young woman and her distended abdomen flattened. Upon examination back at the hospital, the woman's tumors had indeed disappeared, and her vital signs had returned to normal.

Dr. Carrel's response was irreconcilable. "There was no denying that it was distressingly unpleasant to be personally involved in a miracle. . . . It was not a question of accepting some abstract geometric theorem; it was a question of accepting facts which might change the conception of life itself." He chose to write the account of his experience in the third person using the moniker Dr. Lerrac ("Carrel" spelled backward). Perhaps this was his way of illustrating how completely the experience had turned his world upside down, and not just spiritually. He found the courage to bring his account forward to the French scientific community, but he was shunned and ultimately forced to leave France. He found his way to the United States, where, in recognition of his subsequent scientific achievements in the laboratory, he received the Nobel Prize for physiology and medicine.

If the Chimayo story showed me that miracles needed to be looked at from the inside out and not the other way around, the Alexis Carrel story brought me full circle. He is my kinda guy, and not just because I'd invite him into the Doubting Thomas Club if he were still alive. He found his experience "distressingly unpleasant."

He didn't want it to be true, because that meant he had to change who he thought he was. It's risky to talk about a miracle experience, for fear of what rational people might think—even without your livelihood and professional reputation on the line. Any miracle experience, as a gift from God, should be shared, and I admire Dr. Carrel for doing just that in spite of what it cost him initially.

His story is the Perfect Storm as miracle stories go, appealing to my preference for "more is more." You've got the skeptical man of science who is so overwhelmed by what he sees that he is converted; the idea that miracles create faith like the quote from the Archbishop in Shaw's play suggests. Where before Dr. Carrel describes an overriding "feeling of being compressed in too narrow a space," now he is compelled by virtue of his metamorphosis to risk his livelihood and reputation to bear witness to his experience. His faith bursts forth, a wide-open cosmic shift. Additionally, you have the recipient of the miraculous healing, the young woman Marie Bailly, whose great faith in making the journey to Lourdes in such a compromised physical condition becomes a modern-day version of the hemorrhaging woman from the Gospel, and certainly recalls my friend Artie Boyle. In the stories of Marie and Artie, possessing great faith in the first place seems to have brought on the miracle, or at least had something to do with it. Finally, there is the place itself, Lourdes, like holy shrines from all over the world where God's presence seems somehow concentrated and clear.

Trying to capture the definition of a miracle, I felt a little like Sherlock Holmes. I have my clues, however tentative they may be. Faith seems to be a good thing, though God seems willing to pluck some of us out of our flailing complacency and give us a break too. That's unconditional love for you. Praying seems to be a good thing as well; but how many untold stories are out there where the prayers were fervent and maybe even took place after a long journey to a sacred place, and no miracle happened?

The simplest definition would say that a miracle is "an interference with Nature by supernatural power": the spinning sun of

Fatima, saviors appearing out of nowhere, sparks flying as tumors disappear, and of course some irrefutable witness like the skeptic Alexis Carrel validating an inexplicable cure. Meb and Joan are too evolved to require the fireworks that I need in a story. There's not much room in this definition for "the gracious purposive activity of a higher order," the idea that somehow, someway, we are where we are supposed to be, connected to each other and the great Beyond.

We could always count on Joan to give us a shot in the arm when the conversation got sidetracked by Meb, who didn't need a definition to know what miracles were, or bogged down by me and my rules of engagement. If I were the fireworks junky, Joan was still happily insecure: "Let's see what everybody else has to say." Just like she'd done with Blaise Pascal, she brought another library buddy, the Danish philosopher Søren Kierkegaard, to our miracle meeting. He developed the simplest definition of a miracle in a way that brought clarity for all of us. Like the earliest Christians, he considered a miracle a sign, and he used a nautical marker to illustrate his point that a miracle is "a sign only for one who knows that it is a sign, and in the strictest sense only for one who knows what it signifies." For someone who doesn't know what they're looking for, the blinking beacon is just a pretty sight, if you don't know which side is safe and where the channel leads. With big, showy, two-by-four miracles, it's easy to get the sign (unless you're like me), but coincidences require us to be aware, open to the tap on the shoulder.

The day my father died, my brother and I went to the cemetery to pick out a plot. As the man showed us the availability on a map, he came to one on a grassy knoll, and my brother and I looked at each other, interrupted the guy, and said "This is the one we want." He consulted his sheet and announced, "Good, fine. Number 41." Given that 41 was the number of my parents' street address, we knew we'd picked correctly! More than a year later, Jim and I were moving from an apartment to a new home, driving somewhere on an errand, when I burst into tears. I was pregnant with Laura and maybe suffering from serious hormone rage when I blurted out,

"What if Dad doesn't know where I am? I mean, we lived at the apartment when he died. What if he can't find me now?" Raging hormones, irrationality, and tears do not invite the most endearing reaction. Fortunately for me—and for Jim—his response was not the obvious "Are you crazy, Katie?" He commiserated with me and seemed to understand my distress. The next day, a man knocked on the door of our new townhouse to give us our personal code for the outside gate of the development: 41.

If I had known Meb back then, she would have told me that a coincidence is a sign, a potential miracle in disguise, a connection to the spiritual plane Eric told us about that's always there and somehow extends forward and backward in space and time to the "one true God." As we speed through life even the smallest miracle can make us stop and listen, reminding us that all the noise and busyness we create is just the sideline. We belong to a bigger pattern than we can imagine, and sometimes the picture becomes clear, if only for a moment. I used to joke in asking: if a miracle happens in the forest and there is no one around to see it, is it still a miracle? If there's no one to recognize the sign, to claim it as her own, then no meaning can be found. There is no meeting God if we don't engage. For most of my life, I let the signs pass me by.

No one demonstrated the importance of miracles as signs better than Francesco Forgione, a twentieth-century mystic and saint. More commonly known as Padre Pio, he was known to bi-locate and levitate, and he also suffered the stigmata (the wounds of Jesus); but most importantly, he was known as a "reader of hearts" for his ability to see into the soul of another. His greatest achievements were not found in the outward signs of his tremendous feats, but in his commitment to the confessional, to reconciling and reconnecting people with God, and to the relief of their suffering one confession at a time. To have him hear your confession was a sought-after privilege. People would line up at all hours of the day and night to have the opportunity to speak with him. Certainly the three of us would have wanted to join them, if we'd had the chance. A field trip to sunny

Italy is one we could've gotten even Meb to go on—but, alas, he died in 1968.

The three of us had latched onto Padre Pio almost from the beginning of our Chase. He's Italian, so Joan had him at the top of her prayer list, or so I thought. Meb liked what she called "the accoutrements of miracles," and Padre Pio had these in abundance: Stigmata! Bilocation! Levitation!

As if our colored markers on big white paper in Joan's living room weren't enough, at one miracle meeting we had Show and Tell too.

"Katie, I have something for you," Joan said as she mysteriously left the room. When she returned, she was holding out her hand to me.

"It's a holy card and relic of Padre Pio!" Joan responded to the quizzical look on my face (I never pretended to be as steeped in Catholic lore as Joan).

"You just happen to have a relic of Padre Pio in your pocket?" I said as I examined the old holy card.

"My grandmother and her family in Italy loved him, and she gave this to me before she died. I've kept it in my wallet for years," Joan explained. "Besides I've always wanted to know his be-in-two-places-at-once secret."

"So it's all about the multi-tasking and not about the praying. You're human after all," I kidded her.

"Just imagine, Joan, you could be like one of those Sufi whirling dervishes and take bilocation to a whole new level," Meb mused.

"Oh no, I saw those guys in action once and they didn't whirl at all; it was more like slow turning for hours—it would be torture to me!" Joan told us.

"I bet his mysterious feats were well documented. I mean this all happened in the twentieth century. . . ." I looked at Joan, who clearly seemed to know that wasn't the point.

I miss those early days in Joan's living room, though now I understand—Padre Pio's accoutrements got people's attention, but as a healer of hearts and souls, the real action occurred out of sight. In 1947, he heard the confession of a young Polish priest, Karol

Wojyla, and, though it was certainly impossible to see this at the time, declared that the priest would one day become pope. How appropriate it was that this same priest presided over Padre Pio's canonization in 2002 in his role as Pope John Paul II.

All of the stories, the research, and the clues led us to find the most basic definition lacking. Fortunately, an interesting thing happened while the three of us were off chasing our miracle passions: we came up with a definition we all could agree on.

During one of Joan's visits back to California, all of us drinking tea this time and sitting on the barstools in my kitchen, Meb jumped up and started unfolding our original flipchart pages, wondering aloud what we had set out to accomplish and what we were missing.

"We clearly were pretty broad in exploring miracles in other religions," said sleuth Joan, looking at the big pages Meb was attempting to spread across the table and floor.

"Did we decide to forgo a chapter on Truth?" Meb half-shouted, her back turned as she unfolded still more of the large pages. "Because that would have to be a whole other chase, if you ask me."

Then we all laughed as Meb held up the last page she was unfolding—the first page that we ever did. Defining a miracle was right near the top of the list.

We were so close by now, having researched such a broad body of information that, like the perfect fit of the final piece of the puzzle, the definition was right in front of us.

"Miracles have to unfold, in a good way," said Meb.

"They are communications," said Joan, "signs and wonders."

"They have to be divine interventions," I added, as we had become aware of demonic interventions, especially in stories from ancient cultures.

Then, there it was:

A miracle is a sign of divine intervention in the world that creates an unfolding and beneficial connection between God and humankind.

All that effort, energy, and connectedness finally paid off. Our definition made the idea of "miracle" dynamic and ongoing, not unlike our own spiritual journeys. The Ripple Effect, as Meb likes to call it. Magnanimous miracles like the resurrection of Jesus or the Native American concept of nature can be found in this definition, and so can the eerie coincidence that affects one life. Most importantly, the Ripple Effect connects the dots between the experience itself and what happens next and after that and so on until, in Meb's words of wisdom, "it returns to the shores of the eternal."

There is nothing resembling the awe-inspiring or soul-disturbing personal experience of a miracle in a mere definition. After all, when the question "What exactly is a miracle?" is posed, people don't wait to hear the answer before they want to hear or tell the stories. It is the stories that carry the power, as they have for millennia. In the end, I realize that trying to define "miracle" is like trying to catch a beam of light—you can't contain it: and if you could, the light would be extinguished.

In my attempt to define the indefinable, I am aware of how far I have come in the chase—the three of us together, the whole, became greater than the sum of our parts. We had different ideas, pursued different interests, and were waylaid for lengths of time by personal crises; but in the end we were together, each better equipped than before in bringing clarity and a bit of wisdom to the elusive miracle and what it means.

A few years ago, as I strolled around the Harvard Square area during Laura's first semester there, I came across the following verse etched into a stone wall:

God is in the midst of the city.
—Psalm 46

I know Kierkegaard never meant that we should look for literal signs, and I wasn't doing that; but in spite of my best efforts, maybe literal is just what I am sometimes. This was random, refreshing; and as I thought about what it meant, I kept on walking.

On my next trip back to Cambridge, I looked for the sign again. I knew it was important; it had stopped me in my tracks, after all. I just couldn't remember exactly what it had said. Something about God being present, a reminder I knew I needed to carry in my back pocket. But I couldn't find the sign—too many narrow side streets and too easy to lose my way. For a while everything looked the same. I continued my search over my next few visits, refusing to give up. When I finally came across the inscription again, I realized it was as good a reminder of miracles for me as there ever was. How often it seems we stumble over and ignore the signs of God's presence all around us. As I read the sign again, and committed it to memory, I understood why I couldn't stop until I found it. For who better to know that God is indeed in the midst of the city than I?

13

WAVES OF GRACE

If there is a way out of this world;
It is not in darkness;
But here; at the junction of the blues;
Where stars no one asked for;
Strike like miracles.

—DAVID LONG

MEB

A miracle is often associated with asking God to say "yes" to us; like when the quarterback throws the Hail Mary pass, tossing the prayer and the football simultaneously into the heavens, we ask for that one long-shot attempt that we hope will save the game. But miracles are just as often about saying "yes" to God. God can work through us, too. Sometimes miracles happen when we show up as ourselves and do what we can, when we can, and the world is made a better place by our simply being who we are meant to be. In these cases, both the provider and the recipient must say "yes" with faith, not knowing how far the yes will take them, because, like Lewis says, one never knows what you are in for after that. Sometimes these small "yeses" become big ones over time. The way a miracle unfolds usually takes a series of yeses; and so it has been in my life.

The high school Katie's daughters attended is a private school in Oakland, California, some ten miles away from where we both lived. On bended knee, I had gone there years earlier, asking the Head of School to consider accepting my daughter.

He responded thoughtfully, "We've never had a student who

is blind before, and Liz would have to qualify and go through the process."

He knew me from my child-advocacy work and did not think I was neurotic when I began to cry, pleading with him: "I know this is the place for her spirit; please help us keep it alive!"

Liz got her shot—he let her apply, she tested, interviewed and was accepted. I don't know where my daughter would be today if she hadn't been a student there. After Andrew went there as well and hearing me sing the school's praises, Katie knew it was the place she wanted to send her own daughters. In time, College Prep became one of Katie's causes, and it benefited from my friend's impressive financial and fund-raising savvy. We don't always know how things will turn out when we say "yes."

Still, a good story grabs your attention in a way that makes you want to know more about what happens to the characters—what happens after the book or the movie ends. I am the kind of person who wants to know the ending first: you know, the one who reads the last chapter before reading very far into the book. I relax, knowing that it all works out, knowing the worst, or at least knowing what is. What I know, I can accept: it's the suspense that kills me.

I confess a need to understand, to know not just what the outcome will be, but also whether the day-to-day trials and tribulations, joys, and magic moments of my life will add up to something. I have had a hard time putting my journey to paper; it makes it so definite, so real. Carrying the story in my head and heart means that I am still working on it.

As we chased miracles, I sent Katie and Joan volumes of material about Padre Pio, about Fatima and Medjugorje, saints who could fly, stigmata, relics, miracle workers of all times, Christian and otherwise, from my meanderings. One exploration led to another, taking me deeper as I learned more, but never to the ending. As Pierre Teilhard de Chardin said, "We have ever more perfect eyes in a world in which there is always more to see."

Joseph Campbell writes about the story of the hero in myth

and miracle lore who goes on a journey that takes him from home, past a dangerous threshold, into new, challenging territory, then back home again. I love reading about the saints and hearing stories about miracles. I especially love the part about how the real-life characters find home again—a life purpose, a deeper connection with family and friends, an intimate connection with God, even Heaven.

The who-I-am at this moment is tied so much to the who-I-want-to-be. I find guidance in another story of a Wonder Woman who intrigues me. She is a modern-day hero, a tiny figure in a large world: Mother Teresa of Calcutta. You can spend years pondering the meaning of life, or take a moment and read what Mother Teresa said about living. I am determined to expand my mother's motto to include some help from others, and tape a quote attributed to Mother Teresa on my refrigerator:

> *Life is an opportunity. Benefit from it. Life is beauty. Admire it. Life is a DREAM. Realize it. Life is a challenge. Meet it. Life is a duty. Complete it. Life is a game. Play it. Life is a promise. Fulfill it. Life is sorrow. Overcome it. Life is a song. Sing it. Life is a struggle. Accept it. Life is a tragedy. Confront it. Life is an adventure. Dare it. Life is luck. Make it. Life is life . . . Live it.*

Although Mother Teresa hasn't been dead for very long, people are already calling her a saint. I imagine this is how early saints came into being, before there were rules about such things. Just like Augustine, Mother Teresa does not seem perfect to me, and it's comforting to know that saints don't have to be perfect. Once I start reading about her, it seems that I encounter her everywhere: in sermons at church, in books I pick up, even at a fundraiser for Guide Dogs for the Blind.

The Guide Dog event was held in the heart of Napa Valley, which, in my opinion, has a big philanthropic heart. It was a beautiful, abundant fall day, crisp and red-orange with the vines changing color. People were in fine spirits. Outside the main auction hall, where we would later dine and then bid on fabulous vacation destinations, hard-to-find specialty wine, and artwork, I started up a conversation at one of the outdoor tables with an Indian doctor who I knew to be a potential donor. As we sipped the delicious donated wine and ate tiny, delicate appetizers from the area's fabulous restaurants, he asked me what I did for a living. At these times, I stand there perplexed for a moment, thinking to myself, "Really, what *do* I do for a living?" After Bob took the position as the president and CEO of Guide Dogs for the Blind, I had become by default the "wife of the CEO." I had my role in front of me and knew I should interject something about being involved with the organization, the good work done, and the impact it makes in the lives of the blind. Feeling a little rebellious, not wanting to start this just yet, I ventured that I was currently writing a book on miracles. He brightened and said that he had had an interesting experience in India that he could share with me.

Eager to change the subject from dutiful living, and delighted to have a chance to find out something my cohorts hadn't about miracles, I urged him to tell. I could feel a good story coming on.

"I met Mother Teresa."

Part of me was surprised; Mother Teresa seemed pretty far away from this grand Napa fundraiser. But she was popping up everywhere, so I just chuckled inside and asked him, "What was she like?"

"Not what you expect," he said, shaking his head in disbelief. "I think she is a saint."

I was excited. A man who had touched a saint stood before me. Forget the dogs. He was dying to share his story, and I wanted to hear everything. I nodded. "Go on. . . ."

"Well, I had decided I wanted to help, so I contacted her. I told her I would raise the money and I would build a clinic for her. I wanted to help her care for the people of the streets. Know what she said? She said, 'No, thank you.'"

I was surprised. "No, thank you? Did she say why not?" I asked. I had never heard of any nonprofit turning down a big donation.

"She said this was not how God wanted her to do her work. She said that her sisters were charged with going out and caring for people wherever they found them; where they lived, how they lived, where life had taken them. Into the gutter. Into the street. Into the brothels. Wherever and whenever they met someone in need; that was where they were to work. It was not her way to make people come to her."

"That is someone who has thought about their calling and translated it into action based on values," I said. I wished all leaders could be so clear. It was beginning to feel like a message I needed to hear at this moment.

"I thought she was being stubborn and silly. So I built the clinic anyway," he went on, waving his hand as if this was just a small detail. "And you know what she did?" he asked, still clearly dumbfounded. "She refused to make it a hospital or clinic. That tough little nun moved the sisters in there. It became the home for the sisters! So now, her sisters go out and meet people where they are and how they are and where they live. I just built them a clinic for a house to do it from!"

He shook his head. "Saints can be like that, you know," he said, eating a salmon appetizer made by Thomas Keller of the French Laundry. He shrugged his shoulders like he had met many saints but was still amazed by saintliness.

Just then, a volunteer puppy-raiser walked by with the cutest little black lab in her arms, reminding me of the time when my son Andrew raised a guide-dog puppy. She turned and smiled at us, and the puppy wagged his little black lab tail and squirmed as if to get a better look at the two of us. Those eyes would look into the eyes of a blind person some day, and the dog would lead someone like my daughter in a miracle of partnership unlike any other.

I looked around at the graduates with their guides, the donors, the puppy-raisers, the guide-dog trainers, the volunteers. Where was my calling? Where was my guide? "Chin up, girlfriend," I told myself. "You will figure out what comes next. 'Bloom where you are planted.' This is your life too."

"Let's go make a miracle happen at the auction," I said to him, turning to join the larger group. And that the Indian doctor did, bidding up a storm, buying several auction items. The organization was delighted with his generous gifts to them. They weren't about to say no.

Things should have been good with my life; I felt that the story of our Miracle Unfolding had continued. When his consulting company ran into trouble, I was convinced that the "one in a million" job Bob took to support the blind through Guide Dogs was another example of how the ripple effect of our miracle impacted our lives and the lives of others in positive ways. Still, a distance between us remained. After years of Bob spending so much time on the road, this distance was familiar, and so I didn't think much more of it. Now, his travel schedule and workaholism were steady, more predictable; but the focus on the job—clearly connected to the events of our lives—seemed part of the miracle unfolding and seemed justified. I rationalized his behavior, reminding myself that God expects much when He gives much. So I kept my chin up, focused on the kids and their activities and my advocacy work, and continued to repeat my mantra: "Work like everything depends . . ." blah, blah, blah. I was knee-deep in alligators, but I didn't want to know it.

As my friend Maryanne would later tell me, "Girl, you were asleep." Perhaps one can get lulled asleep by a Miracle.

So, just when I thought I could relax and trust the sense of love and grace that comes with having a miracle unfold, just when I was beginning to let a little fun and joy back into my life and bear witness to God's love for me, I got a wakeup call. I am forced to admit that I do not get to dictate the end of the story.

Quite by accident, I find out Bob is having an affair. The ground shifts. This scene does not fit with my plan of how our

Miracle will unfold. I am devastated and ashamed. I have lost my voice. I tell no one.

I don't give up—that's not who I am. I work hard to make sense of this new twist in my life, even as I try to forgive Bob and move forward. Admittedly, I don't do a very good job of forgiving him. It is very hard to love myself right now. Staying with him makes it feel like there's something in me crumbling every day, but leaving means giving up and letting the "bad guys" win. I try to focus on being able to turn things over to God; maybe I don't have to hold it all up by myself all the time. This feeling of walking with Someone by my side is something I call Hope. I imagine Hope believes in me, even if, right now, I do not. I write in my journal:

Hope is walking with me
Pushing me to take the next step.
So I do. I lift my foot,
feel the pain and the weight of it—
Push myself to put it down in a solid place.
Hope smiles.
She says, "Now the next step."

Sometimes, after a bad day, I lose Hope.
She runs ahead of me and I can't keep up.
Then the darkness comes, and, for a while,
I am lost.

In the morning,
Hope is back with the dawn.
She lets me know she is there by touching my heart.
She tells me she's found a new way to go

In the evening,
We laugh and cry together, reviewing the day

Where we were and where we will go tomorrow
We tell each other stories about what matters most.

With Hope,
I know the sun will always rise.
Right there—
Between the mountains.

On the spring morning when Bob told me that he wanted to leave, I prayed to Mary for a miracle, just as hard and as much in despair as I had on the night in the hospital with Liz. This time, there was no stranger telling me all would be well. To me, the story of trauma is not only what happens initially, but what one does with the situation after, and apparently Bob had previously found solace from the pressures of our life outside our family home. As the truth of his choices unfolded, my heart was breaking; but if he had said he wanted to try again, I would have: I believe in miracles that much. I hadn't learned yet that to really experience the sense of love and grace that comes with having a miracle unfold, I had to love myself first.

I always thought that when Liz was independent, when we got the kids launched, when Bob was more secure and less frantic about his work (do you see the When-Then pattern?), we would spend our "quality time" having fun together, sharing the life we had planned all those years ago when we were first married. Without the pressures of raising kids, the complications of the blind world, and the frustrations of the calendar that always seemed to be full of commitments, we would focus again on just the two of us. We had worked hard, but we were worn out. I begged him to embrace our life together; to be patient, stay, and wait for the goodness of the Lord. He chose otherwise.

Stubborn and determined, confident that with enough prayer and hard work I could achieve anything, I tried everything to get him back. We went on walks, I cooked him the dinners he loved, I accommodated his work schedule and trips cheerfully. I even bought a new nightgown. He struggled, I think, with this "angelic" Meb and wavered between what he thought could be a heavenly existence with someone else and the life we had together, which was raw and required responsibility and strength on a daily basis.

There was a further problem, and I knew it: this woman fighting for her marriage was not me. One afternoon, I'd had it. I was angry that Bob was never available to help me take care of things around the house. Daniel was at football practice, and Bob was "working." The dryer wasn't drying again, and I decided to fix it myself. I jumped up on the dryer, wearing my slippery yoga outfit, and reached down behind the dryer to disconnect it from the vent, checking to see if the vent was clogged. Suddenly my weight shifted, and I slid down head-first between the wall and the back of the dryer, my head stuck right next to the disconnected exhaust with the dryer still on. I was trapped; there was no way to leverage myself back up again. Panic ensued. My head pounded. I felt dizzy with heat and the gas. I pictured myself dying in the laundry room, my head and upper body hidden, my feet sticking out like the Wicked Witch of the East, found days later by either Bob or Daniel. Upside down, gasping for air, I thought about the true miracles in my life. I wasn't perfect and I wanted a deeply committed, passionate marital relationship with Bob. After twenty-seven years, I refused to believe that we could not make it so. In all honesty, I had held on, really thinking all would be well. With all my strength, I found a handhold on the side of the the washing machine, and by squirming and slowly walking myself up the wall, I shifted my weight until I could finally slide off the machine. Shaking, I went and sat down on the couch in the family room.

I knew that if the Divine can use difficulty and darkness for good, then free will allows the Profane to use difficulty and darkness for evil. One can find moments in life where the fulcrum is placed perfectly, where a nudge either way can shift the balance in one direction or another. So it felt in my life right at that moment. I prayed with all my heart for a miracle to guide me.

But it always takes two, and Bob was finished. I suppose there comes a time for any optimist when the writing is on the wall and denial is no longer an option. For me, the ending of my marriage came this way. It was prolonged and sudden at the same time, both cliché and uniquely dramatic: an affair; an attempt at forgiveness; another affair; angry words; lonely nights; an Indian shaman on a trip Bob took without me, where he saw The Truth and was led by his own angels; a trip to our home in Mendocino where I thought we would celebrate our anniversary and reconnect; and Bob came just to say good-bye. It would take me another year to allow myself to believe he would never be back.

In the meantime, God would send me small miracles to light my way.

Liz graduated from Stanford with honors and was accepted into a graduate school for a PhD in Philosophy. After her graduation, we decided to celebrate by treating ourselves to a spa weekend, something we had never done before. In fact, neither of us had received many massages or other spa-like treatments, so we were charting new territory in self-care together. We signed up for the gamut: a psychic reading, ayurvedic massage, yoga, hiking, water therapy, and an excursion with horses.

What can it be but God's grace that allows a wife to let go in peace? The experience of being cared for so exquisitely at this spa just outside Tucson, Arizona, from their support and unconditional acceptance of Liz and her guide dog, to the physical and emotional support we received during various programs, all gave me permission to actually *feel* what it's like to be cared for. It was during a massage where I allowed myself to let go and enjoy the experience, to free myself of all that came up and out of me, that I knew I could make Bob's leaving very hard, or I could be graceful about it—a dancer. I had learned as a ballerina in my youth that movement never lies. As I let go of the grief and pain I had held for so long inside, I told myself I would dance my heart and I would not stop him this time. He could quit his job, be with his "new family" and start all over again;

free of the disappointments, the grief, sadness and pain, the loss of what might have been, the loss of what was never done. I didn't agree with his choices, but I would not choose to devalue myself again. Somehow, God gave me that strength. I took the road less traveled, at least for me. I set out to learn to love myself.

So, what does it mean to move on? I remember that this is what doctors, family, and friends said after Liz was abused. Move on.

"Get a move on" is different. Get a move on implies a quickening of the body. Action. When I tell one of my kids to get a move on, it means hurry up, speed into action, keep up with the group. I do much better at getting a move on than moving on.

What if I don't want to move on? What if I am not finished with processing Right Now? I feel pushed from behind when someone says "move on," judged in some way, as if I am not taking the right action: that, from the speaker's viewpoint, I am stuck.

Maybe I am. Some say I was stuck in an unhealthy marriage. Some tell me I am stuck with a blind kid. Stuck with no job and few job prospects. Stuck living a life I never imagined nor, at least consciously, set out to attain. Joan offered me some comfort and understanding that maybe being stuck, at least temporarily, is okay. Maybe I'm stuck because I haven't used all the juice here in the present; I haven't wrung out everything that is important to learn. Maybe "stuckness" is there for a reason. What if I still love?

I cannot stop another from moving on. Of this I am certain. I don't want to spend my time setting up roadblocks, but I reserve the right to stay in my place while someone else gets a move on in their life. I relish the dragging of my feet, if only to grieve, to mourn, to sort the good from the bad, so that I know what to take with me when I get up and go. Painfully, I realize a fundamental truth about human nature: when someone tells you who they really are, Believe Them.

A year later, there is another miracle.

I am in the church courtyard after the morning's service, having coffee, when my very Christian friends Woody and Julie come by to say hi. They tell me they are happy to see me and ask how I am. I tell them, honestly, "I am not doing very well. I am trying to single-parent my rebellious youngest son, who is applying to college and finishing his senior year; I've just sold our family home and have moved to a rented place; and I've started a new retail job after essentially being out of the workforce for twenty-five years."

"There is a lot of collateral damage," Woody commiserates, shaking his head.

Julie tries to comfort me. She gives me a hug and says, in a heartfelt voice, "Meb, remember, God uses everything for good. He does not ask us to do more than we can."

I know she means well, but, just like Katie, I really hate this saying. The idea that God doesn't give us any more than we can handle offends me. I am about ready to retort that "divorce cannot be good and God surely doesn't know how hard it has been on all of us. I am way over my personal limit, and . . ." Suddenly, I feel a hand on my heart; a real presence of Someone's hand on my heart. It calms me. A voice inside me says "God knows you could not have handled what Bob is going to do. You could not have handled the person he is choosing to be. God is looking out for you with this divorce just as surely as He did in the hospital room with Elizabeth."

I am finally ready to let the father of my children—my Wasbund, as I will call him—go.

By now, you know how I really didn't want this to be the ending to our love story. I wanted to be able to say "Look! See the wonder of God in our miracle! Everything worked out . . . the miracle unfolded and, ta-da, all is well. Bob and I live happily ever after into the sunset of our years with grandchildren around in a healthy, happy home."

So many of the questions we miracle-chasers worked on have been present for me this last year. What if the miracle you get is not the one you prayed for? Does God answer all our prayers? What is the purpose of a miracle in one's life? And although, over the years, I have learned much about miracles, I can't honestly tell you that I have answered these questions for myself.

You see, I have chased my miracle thoughts into a corner again, because we all know that God doesn't lie in wait, excitedly anticipating your latest slip-up (as my adolescent children suspected I did). He doesn't put us in difficult circumstances, thinking up bad things that can happen, to make a cosmic point. Bad things do happen, though. And to people I love. I don't have an answer for why, or how to undo them. Maybe there is a miracle about to happen, and maybe there is a miracle we will never know about that does happen. I will continue to pray for one—but any more, I am not sure what to ask. So I just keep my heart channel open and reach with my energy and soul-love out to God, trusting that He knows what I cannot.

I have seen the power of a miracle unfold with my own eyes. I know that without a doubt, the ripple effect of our miracle has had an effect on the unnamed masses: Bob's leadership at Guide Dogs, informed by his experience as the father of a child who is blind; the children and families protected through Trustline, the legislation our family helped support for children with disabilities and victims of Shaken Baby Syndrome; the impact on doctors and lawyers, social workers and teachers touched by Liz's small, strong voice. In my own life, the ripple from our miracle has sometimes sustained me, but at other times has felt like a tsunami threatening to overwhelm my life and carry me off along with it. At these times, I think of others who have glimpsed the miraculous. Bernadette, confident in what she'd seen, who stayed true to her own personal vision, refusing to say the words others kept trying to put in her mouth, even in the face of persecution. Mother Teresa, who received the call to become a nun, only to be called again to become a force for good in Calcutta. Mary, the mother of Jesus, a very young and illiterate woman, who accepted her new reality without really understanding, trusting in God, obedient; even she asks the angel "How can this be?" We miracle recipients are the only real experts on our experience; and it is through fully living our own experience that we give the miraculous the power to change lives far beyond our own. As Mother Teresa said, "You can do something I can't do. I can do something you can't do. Together let us do something beautiful for God."

When Liz was about nine, she and I were hiking together in a forest and I remember her asking me, "Mom, do you think it was a good thing that I got blinded?"

Surprised, I told her honestly, "No, honey. But I think we made good things come out of it."

Rainer Maria Rilke, in *Letters to a Young Poet,* says this:

> Be patient toward all that is unsolved in your heart and try to love the questions themselves. Do not now seek the answers, which cannot be given you because you would not be able to live them. And the point is to live everything. Live the questions.

Here's what I do know: the miracle of Liz's recovery has taught me the important life lesson of living everything. Given my need for security and safety, it seems to be a miracle that I can trust in the unfolding of my life and in the unfolding of God's plan for me, no matter how different or difficult this plan may seem to be from the one I defined for myself.

This week, I have a wonderful reprieve from my empty nest: both my sons are with me in my small new place. When I come home from taking Liz back to graduate school, there isn't a clean plate or bowl or cup in the house. No square foot of floor space without guitars, shoes, clothes, or books. Moving from a very large and beautiful home into this space means stuff is everywhere. I thank God for these two wonderful souls in my life who, with such good cheer, and with only a small touch of apology for the state of the place, welcome me home with open arms.

God has provided for Liz. She is doing what she loves, studying philosophy and teaching. In a few years, she will have her PhD and will be able to influence the ethics and moral values of our society through her work in a university, and through writing and public speaking. Supporting herself with her stipend and fellowship, she lives with a roommate, her cat, and her guide dog. My role is changing from reader, advocate, taxi driver, and personal assistant to recipe-giver, phone problem-solver, and confidante. I welcome the woman she has become; she teaches me something every day.

The spa, called Miraval, was the sanctuary I needed, that rest stop on the Camino, the road of the pilgrimage of Life we travel, that helped me take the breath that allowed me to keep going forward. Mir—as in mirare—to see, to wonder. In Russian, mir means peace. After such an arduous journey, I still refuse to let the "bad guys win," those forces of evil that caused Liz to be blinded in the first place. Having held on to this mantra through the ups and downs of legislation, fights for inclusion, disability rights, and the rocky road at the end of my marriage, it seems disturbing and disappointing to look at the face of evil in my own heart and realize that I am not able to forgive and love Bob the way I want to and still love myself at the same time. I wish Bob well. I admit I miss his love and his friendship. And—because "where there is great love, there are always miracles"—I look forward to finding Great Love again.

It's time for me to create a new nest of my own. Things are so different, so up in the air, I can't begin to tell you the end of my story. Without a doubt, my journey has taught me how to be patient; to work hard, to let go and let God. I have a clearer knowledge of God's presence in my life and I am, at least for now, at a place of peace. As for the next part of my life, Joan found a new mantra for my refrigerator. It may be corny, but I like it anyway:

Dance as though no one is watching you,
Love as though you've never been hurt before,
Sing as though no one can hear you,
Live as though heaven is on earth.
—Souza

Except now I know Someone is always with me.

Even God understands the importance of marking beginnings and endings by taking some time to step back and find perspective. After all, in the beginning of the world, when He or She was finished creating, a well-deserved cosmic rest was taken. It was then that God took a breather and stepped back to appreciate the beauty and perfection of this Creation, when then and only then did it become clear that in the miracle of creation was the exciting—well, probably electrifying, really—unfolding that allowed the stars to shine and the sun to burn, and the tides to turn and the earth to move. Maybe even God was amazed by the power of this Miracle unfolding over time.

So, I think, God just went right on creating. And to this day, when God wants to connect with his creation from time to time, because no artist, dancer, author, inventor—or even a Mother—can ever truly let go of a creation, then God creates another Miracle that speaks to us of His connection with us as it unfolds through time.

Like the ripples in a universal lake, a Miracle is the perfect stone God tosses into the very center of the still more perfect water. When we look, we can see how the ripples cascade across time and space until their energy returns to a distant shore like a wave unto itself. For all is really One.

14

Taking the High Road

Divine Incognito

—Søren Kierkegaard

KATIE

The Ripple Effect Meb talked about from the beginning was now embraced by each of us. It taught me to pay attention to the kinds of spiritual signs I had somehow missed along the way. Sadly, Meb missed the more concrete ones from Bob, not that it made much difference in the end. But Meb never lost her faith; and, though stuck, as she puts it, and alone, she never lost herself either, allowing the three of us to continue our Chase as we had before when the going got tough, though our meetings were now less structured. We snatched whatever three-way phone time we could. During one particularly epic conversation, we decided to revisit any unanswered questions we still had. The big question for me had always been: "Why?" Why do some people get a miracle and others don't?

"Miracles are not *about* you, per se, but about your gift to the world," Meb suggested. "God has given you a gift so that you may share your gift with others. You're a miracle-ee."

"I'm a what? Are we making up our own language now, Meb? 'Cuz if we are, it's definitely time to hang up our miracle cleats!" I implored.

"Katie's really just upset to hear after all this time that it's not all about her," Joan chuckled.

"Anyway," Meb continued, "a miracle-ee doesn't deserve or

not-deserve the answer to a prayer, or a wish, or a miraculous intervention: it's about all of us who benefit from the one who *got* the
miracle in order for the world to receive your gift."

"So it's all about the Ripple Effect," I concluded.

"By George, I think she's got it!" I could feel the gratification in
Meb's voice charging through the phone wires.

As Meb was planning her trip to Miraval and Joan and family
were arranging an exotic excursion to faraway lands, both in search
of closure, I thought about where I could go. Comfortable as I am
in my new miracle shoes, I decided to journey on to Chimayo, New
Mexico, home of the miraculous healing dirt and site of my favorite
miracle story. Chimayo has been called the Lourdes of America,
and if I were going to visit a holy shrine, this seemed like a practical
geographical idea. I had been searching with two college friends
for a spot to celebrate our fiftieth birthdays; and when I suggested
Santa Fe, with full disclosure of my Miracle Chase in mind, they
were game.

Chimayo is located thirty miles north of Santa Fe on the "high
road to Taos." It has been considered holy ground by the Tewa
Indians for centuries. Legend has it that the dirt's healing powers
came from the mud left over from the remnants of an early sacred
pool. In the nineteenth century, long after Catholicism had taken
hold, the story of the sacred Indian ground was replaced by another,
about a special crucifix found near the site where a chapel was eventually built in 1814, Il Santuario de Chimayo. Inside the chapel, in a
small antechamber, is a hole in the ground with the miraculous dirt.

My friends and I arrived in Chimayo on a spectacular fall day,
the kind of day on which you might even expect a miracle, the clear
blue of the Southwest sky unreal in its brilliance. The simple adobe
chapel was sparsely appointed on the inside with lovely primitive-
style panels depicting saints behind the altar and on either side
wall, reflective of the colorful Native American and Spanish influences. As I sat in a front pew, I managed to say a prayer of thanksgiving, but I was anxious to get to the little room with the dirt and

left all too soon for the shop next door to buy my dirt containers. The small clear containers weren't easy to spot in the midst of all the bright, cheap plastic saints and miniature Jesuses. I realized too late that I should have stayed in the chapel—taken my time. By the time I got to the small chamber next to the chapel that contained the dirt, I felt like a touristy voyeur, and the dirt in the ordinary hole in the ground seemed as far away from sacred pools as my backyard in California.

I have had moments where if God had been corporeal, I could have reached out and touched Him. It happened once at Mass as I said a prayer for help from the depths of my being (I'm guessing that's where a person's soul must be) at a time in my life when babies, work, widowed mother, and fractured childhood family had left me in a hidden state of anxiety for so long that I couldn't remember the last time I'd laughed—or cried, for that matter. I had been slowly drowning for years, and there wasn't much air left. I had barely finished my prayer when I felt it, instantaneous and powerful, this strength to become unstuck in my unhealthy status quo of non-decisions. And I changed my life: quit my job, reordered priorities, with my marriage and myself near the top of the list, where before neither had made the top five. I've been close to having that feeling at random other times, like when a deep-pink-streaked sky carries the remnants of the last of the sun's rays and suddenly I feel enveloped in the Creator's embrace, invited into nature's dance, part of the Plan.

But here in Chimayo where I expected a concentration of grace, I felt nothing. Somehow, rather than dashed expectations, I realized for the second time in this Chase that spiritual awareness and connection are propelled from within; unless you're a mystic, these moments of peak divine sensory perception can't be premeditated. The stories of healings from Chimayo aren't diminished because the place somehow failed me (more likely, *I* failed *it*). I had learned from Joan to appreciate the essence of a story, and Chimayo will remain for me a symbol of faith not just for the Catholic populace, but as land identified long, long ago by the first Americans as a sacred place, especially blessed by God.

Someone once asked me where the Chase would end. I thought the answer would be "When we find out all we possibly can": after we'd saturated ourselves with Saints and Wise Guys, peered into the traditions of the tribal and the great religious faiths, examined the personal experiences of the three of us and those of the friends we met along the way, and even occasionally embarking on a real chase—to Fairfax, California; Hingham, Massachusetts; or Chimayo, New Mexico. To chase means to go after something in a hurry. In my case, a frenzied pursuit to grab the low-hanging fruit of miracle lore. It was fun to satisfy my curiosity, and there was enough information out there to keep me skimming the surface indefinitely.

"Did you know St. Paul might have had frontal-lobe epilepsy, and that might be what really happened on the road to Damascus?" I'd announced at one of our early meetings. Meb suggested that that didn't make it less of a miracle, since Paul became one of the most prolific writers on Christianity in history.

"There's this guy Charles Babbage who invented an early computer to prove David Hume's anti-miracle statement wrong. How cool is that?" I'd asked at another meeting. Meb and Joan both peered at me with the collective look (apparently we all occasionally got that from the other two), as if to say "And the point is . . . ?"

"According to Karen Armstrong, Islam was the best of the big three at respecting the others and most enlightened toward women . . . back in the day." This prompted a multi-religious dialogue facilitated by Joan and a bit of Catholic Church bashing because I couldn't help myself.

Then Jim got sick and somehow I couldn't separate that from my father's death. And then Joan got sick and I knew that her life was held in the balance, not just for months but for years. I watched Meb struggle with the reality of everyday life, the ripple of Liz's life that became the miracle but also a tragedy that impacted a family forever. I discovered that you can't just chase miracles to really understand them, and our Chase had become a journey, less random, more thoughtful. We had become seekers of deeper faith and understanding.

Faith wasn't somebody else's for me to admire, but my own. Prayer wasn't the detached admiration I felt for those who did it well—it was offered by me in dusty, halting, begging whispers. I tell myself to be prepared, to do the hard work of faith now when I don't need it, so that someday when I do it will kick in on auto-Katie-pilot. I cringe at the thought of ever needing it again as I remind myself to be wary, to keep it fresh. All too often, I flail about in fits and starts.

This was never better demonstrated than on another trip that Joan had suggested, where miracle-chasing was not supposed to be involved. I should have known—with Joan, no project is ever put down, just suspended in air long enough to catch other responsibilities before they hit the ground, like a master juggler perfecting her craft. Meb and I were not alone in our admiration for Joan's abilities. Her Boston friends wrote a parody on her fiftieth birthday using "The Cat and The Hat" theme about Joan 1 and Joan 2. "Joan number one likes to fundraise and cook, Joan number two is writing a book."

By the time Allie decided to attend Tufts University, following her sister to the Boston area, I had double the reason to visit Joan, and more opportunity to watch her multi-tasking skills up close and personal. It's not surprising that a canoe trip down the Ipswich River to enjoy the fall foliage would be Joan's idea of a nice mental break. Of course, as Joan pointed out, we could also discuss miracles as we paddled merrily along. Never mind that there were two other canoes filled with her friends who were with us, or the tiny little detail that I don't care for water sports of any kind, especially not ones that require any coordination on my part. Canoes are also too small for me to feel good about relinquishing control to someone else. I tried to get out of going, but was loath to be seen as a wimp. It was all about image—I didn't care that I actually was a wimp. Joan insisted that the river was only two feet deep this time of year.

The canoe-rental place was being run this beautiful October morning by the unshaven, gruff Wick, whose potbelly hung out of his wrinkled, unbuttoned shirt. This guy had seen better days. It was hard to tell whether his raspy voice was due to years of heavy smoking or to the terrible cold he announced he had. No burly young man to instill confidence in the sport of canoeing—just Wick, who clearly didn't want to be here any more than I did. When I asked about the river being only two feet deep, he half chuckled and said "In some parts; and in others maybe twenty."

Joan and I got in one of the canoes with her friend Patty, who supposedly would paddle in the back and steer. Joan took the front seat, and I sat cross-legged in the middle. We each had our own paddle. Three paddles might be a good thing if you want to go fast, but it's a bad thing if you end up going in fast circles instead. Or, worse, if you end up canoeing into rocks and logs along the river-bank. Joan reminded us to avoid the fork in the river that led to a waterfall. Within minutes of being in the river, my heart started pounding so loudly that I was sure I would disturb the wildlife. When I voiced how I was feeling, Joan turned around, exasperated. "Katie, what are you afraid of? What is the worst that could happen?" she wanted to know. Of course, I knew the answer to that question: I could fall out of the canoe in the twenty-foot-deep part, be choked and pulled down by riverweed, and drown. I knew not to share this answer with Joan. I just looked at her and decided to get a grip on myself. Be rational, for God's sake, which I am supposedly so goddamn good at. I was really wondering where the pebble in the quiet lake is at this point.

It took the three of us some time to learn to work together. Even though it was Patty's job to steer from the back of the canoe, Joan and I also tried to steer, creating a situation of constant over-correction and banging into things. Eventually we had to let go and have faith in Patty. My panic subsided, of course, as soon as we got the hang of it. Conquering fear and having faith, both prevailing challenges in my life, have much in common. The concept of letting go takes practice for me. I realize that without letting go, faith cannot exist. Maintaining control makes it difficult to expose the soul to the elements. Once I let go, I was able to capture remarkable beauty in the photographs I took of the brilliant fall foliage reflected in the river current.

The Ipswich River canoe trip would be my last adventure with Joan for the Miracle Chase, a journey where I had gained insight about things I never thought to ask about and realized at the same time that some questions will never be fully resolved.

The truth is that I wasn't completely satisfied with Meb's theory about "your gift to the world," though I believed her idea was compelling. It took a tragic accident to reinforce my own feelings that there would be no neat answer to my burning question, "Why?"

A friend's twenty-five-year-old son, Scott, was killed in a motorcycle accident a summer ago. A scholar and star rower at Georgetown University, he followed his passion for the politics of globalization to India, where he met the love of his life and was about to return to England to start a master's program at the London School of Economics. His dad, Frank, and I would commiserate about our children's adventures as we waited for board meetings to begin at College Prep, the high school our children had attended, and Frank's face lit up when describing his son's adventures. Scott was one of those young adults who, it seemed, would somehow alter the landscape of the world. Instead, he died during a last adventure to Turkey when an errant truck driver crossed into the oncoming lane. At the funeral, the priest knew that one question was on all of our minds: Why? How do you absorb the loss of someone so young and with such potential? He suggested that none of us should leave with the idea that this was somehow God's will. "This is not God's will. To have faith," he continued, "we are required to live with the question. The unanswerable question: Why?"

The question is as old as humankind's ability to imagine beyond the stars. The Greeks had the Moirai, three goddesses known as the Fates, who, I think, when they were especially good, were known as the Graces. (I know three women who fit that description.) They were present at a person's birth, responsible for weaving the thread of a person's life, and overseeing, with rare exception, a person's fixed destiny.

In more modern times, Calvin stirred up controversy in his version of predestination, turning us all into automata. No need to worry about a thing, just enjoy the ride—or not, depending on the cards you get dealt. Personally, I prefer Chief Shenandoah and his "It's the path to the Creator. . . . It's the only path there is," a call to be aware of where you're headed, a reminder to rely on your own soulful intuition of getting there one step at a time. It's open, it's customized, and it lets you bang into rocks on occasion, but also leaves you room to right the boat. The point is that a lot of really smart people have been trying to figure out since time immemorial who's pulling the strings and whether we're pulling back or are just puppets in the show.

I like the idea that there is a plan, but I'm guessing that if God has a plan for me, then there are plans for each of us, and none of the plans include violent, untimely death. As soon as you go down the road of "It's A Wonderful Life," the lives I've helped create, or touched, or befriended or sustained as being a piece of the answer, you must wrestle with the lives unlived, the lives untouched, the potential ones that evaporated in tragedy. As soon as you say "I lived because . . . ," you resurrect the magic-wand-waving god who says "yes" to me and "no" to someone else. At the same time, each of us does touch, love, accomplish the great and the small; and these things do have meaning. In the immortal words of Shakespeare, "There's the rub."

I found comfort in Euripides: "What if death be that which men call life, and life what men call death?" What if death is full of the overwhelming peace that Artie felt on the mountaintop when he didn't care if God took him right at that moment, not so much as a good-bye to the wife and kids? One moment with the Divine and he was content to take an immediate exit. Thomas Aquinas and

Blaise Pascal had their own encounters, as Joan discovered, and then couldn't wait for their curtain call. We all have read about the near-death experience, where the person sees what's on the other side and isn't always thrilled about coming back. We're stuck with the knots on the back side of the tapestry. On the other side, the exquisite side, in the realm of the complexity of God, is where the young women Ted Bundy murdered can be found. I have to believe that.

Maybe "Why?" is the wrong question. Maybe the question should be "How?" How do we love better, believe better, appreciate better? These are questions we can answer, where we control (finally!) the ability to seize the day. It reminds me of the serenity prayer my youngest sister, Mary, recites every day at her AA meetings: "God grant me the serenity to accept the things I cannot change; the courage to change the things I can; and the wisdom to know the difference." She also taught me a thing or two about taking a leap of faith.

Mary was nineteen, a college student away from home, when my father died, and she more than the rest of us felt the full weight of our family's dissolution. If a little alcohol eased the pain, then a lot of alcohol made it disappear. It didn't happen overnight—like most alcoholics, the train wreck was in slow motion. Six years ago, struggling as a single mom with two daughters, she checked herself into an intensive outpatient treatment program. Thirty days out, her newfound sobriety bubble burst. Alone in her house, the craving she felt overtook her being, clamoring so loudly in her head that ending the deafening noise was all that mattered. Shaking, she tried to save herself with a call to her sponsor. No answer. Then a call to one of her treatment "mates." No answer. She had been told in treatment that she was on a spiritual path now and, as a last gasp, decided to say a really short prayer she knew from Anne Lamott, the only one she could hear in her pounding head: "Help me, help me, help me." (I guess being a fan of Anne Lamott runs in my family.)

Instantly, a scene from an Indiana Jones movie came into her head as vividly as if she were watching it, though it had been more than ten years since she'd seen it. On his way to retrieve the Holy Grail in order to save his father's life, Indiana has already heroically made it past the first two hurdles, when he finds himself on a slim ledge overhanging a gigantic canyon. He is grasping the wall of rock behind him in order not to fall forward, but finds nothing to hang on to. He has no choice but to do the hardest, scariest thing of all: he takes a giant step off the ledge into mid-air. Just as you're sure he will fall to his death, part of a bridge appears. With each step, more bridge, and so on, until he makes it to the other side. My sister tells the rest better than I can:

"Okay, God, I get the metaphor. Thanks for the help. I felt the craving subside, my sponsor called back, and I went about my day without picking up a drink. That night as I crawled into bed, I thought about this whole higher-power thing being more real than Santa Claus. I flipped on the TV. I surfed two channels, and my jaw dropped open as I landed on the third. There was Harrison Ford. I watched the scene unfold just as it had in my mind only hours before. He gets to the ledge, and I watch the bridge appear under his boot."

Mary has stayed sober since. As she said, "I learned not to quit five minutes before the miracle happened."

Some people never have to take that leap of faith. Others, like me, have to take the leap to get to the other side where all the pieces fit together. At the beginning of this journey, I was stuck in what I called the land of in-between; in between skeptic and believer, in between the serial killer and the angel, one foot on the ground beneath my feet and the other wanting to step off the cliff. They were equal in my mind, the ghost and the angel, dangling reason and spirit as if I had to choose between them. Now, ten years later, I'm no longer in the land of in-between. I can live with the unanswerable question. While I will never stop recognizing terrible suffering as part of the human condition, I have a different view from the other side of the canyon. This may not sound like much, but for me it's profound. I'm a believer without the "but" at the end of the sentence.

15

MAGICAL MIRACLE TOUR

In my end, is my beginning.

—T. S. ELIOT

JOAN

It's great to have friends once your children grow up, because your friends, with their own surprising revelations, will fill in the gaps left by your children's incessant questioning. It's hard to imagine that after ten years of soul-searching, Meb, Katie, and I would have anything new to talk about. Then Katie drops a bombshell, describing her total discouragement with balancing the roles of employee, mother, wife, and citizen of the world. No surprise there; it's hard, really hard to balance everything, especially when you want to get them all right. Katie is our "bottom line" person (she can't help herself), but she can also wax poetic about a sunrise, the mountain glow at sunset, or even the perfect french fry. However, experiencing a visceral sensation in church (no less), prompting her to change her life? No Way. To most who know her, that scenario alone would qualify as a miracle. Ironically, to Meb and me, it's not.

We were with Katie as she broadened her horizons exponentially, from judging miracles within a prescribed and narrow scope, to her willingness to see shades of gray. Meb and I both recognized the sensation she felt as one more example of not being Alone. It's a step along a path we each begin when we see that we are being called to engage in our own life's story, to make choices and take charge. And here's the big "and": it's all right. Not the St. Julian "all right," but the *all right* that comes with the encouragement of your friends and family, those who trust and believe in you.

Meb has carried on and gotten here, too. Difficult as it is, it is no particular surprise that her marriage with Bob dissolved. Once Elizabeth was abused, the odds of remaining together were stacked against them. Still, I am not one of those people who say "It's for the best; he wasn't good enough for her after all." I liked Bob. I even thought they made a good pair, each of them refusing to accept a simple explanation when a penetrating, mind-altering one could be found. Although I was her friend, I never understood how much energy it took to look at life that way—and how hard it was for Meb to relax. I was sad for my friend—cried, in fact—when I pieced together the broken pieces of her shattered dreams. A couple of years ago, in an e-mail, Meb told us:

> It is a miracle, but I started writing again. I got the "papers" from Bob and hired a lawyer and suddenly, there is space. Do you still want me?

As if Katie and I would ever not want our friend! But we understood: this is how you feel when your world caves in around you.

> All is transition at this time. I never was good with transitions. Pray for me and please, oh please, bear with me. I've never done this before.

Now, a few years later, it's good to see Meb move past the losses in her life. She has resurfaced and emerged, like her daughter, "full of promise, full of hope."

It's funny: Katie is the one who always wanted to feel more comfortable in her skin, but Meb is the one who is. She is finding the remarkable woman she is inside—the one she feels she had lost—reconnecting with her authentic self, some might say. Lord knows, it hasn't been easy to go from the idealized life in suburbia to the reality of her life at this moment. Capable, understanding and empathetic, Meb knows what needs to be done in her new professional role working to help other families across California who have children with disabilities, and she cherishes the respect she garners from those she supports. I know, in time, all will be well for Meb; she, too, has realized she is not Alone. Katie would say it's refreshing. I say it's miraculous.

We teased Meb during the ten years of our writing together that she was our Tao, where knowing was in the unknowing, an elusive concept for more traditional thinkers like Katie and me. If Katie and I teased Meb, it came right back at me. They call me the Energizer Bunny—I do keep going and going. It keeps me engaged, my life new at every moment—it's how I feel comfortable. It's also one of the ways I try to get things to make sense. I can't rest until I figure out not only a rationale for how things work, but also to plan the next steps. I had known we shouldn't have opened that enticing Box of Pandora, ever since I had recognized the Death by Miracle theme dancing on the wings of the Wise Guys; but like so many before us, how could we refuse? Fortunately, as we lived the journey contained in these pages, I was reassured by the wisdom contained in Joseph Campbell's words:

> This brings us to the final crisis of the round, to which the whole miraculous excursion has been but a prelude, that, namely, of the paradoxical, supremely difficult threshold-crossing of the hero's return from the mystic realm into the land of common day. Whether rescued from without [Katie], driven from within [Meb] or gently carried along by the guiding divinities [Joan], he has yet to re-enter with his boon the long-forgotten atmosphere where men who are fractions imagine themselves to be complete.

After ten years of chasing miracles, we returned to the "land of common day" with a better understanding of the experiences that shaped our lives and made us stronger. Katie exercised a faith that had always been there, but now she understands it for the gift it is; Meb found a new beginning where grief has slowly dissipated with each passing day, and her own dynamic spirit has resurfaced; I discovered my indomitable heart and, for the first time, can breathe a sigh of relief knowing I really am a survivor. The "boon" of my "miraculous excursion" is a renewed faith in God, in each other, and in myself. Sharing our stories has been a way to put a personal name and face to the ethereal and the presence of the Almighty in our lives today. With our re-entry almost complete, we feel carried by that intrinsic spirit, "the guiding divinities," certain that something greater is at work and willing to tell our stories to others.

The Chinese proverb was right: the journey of a thousand miles did begin with the simplicity of a single step. In the experiences we shared, we kept moving forward, both in our quest and in our lives, by continuing to put one foot in front of the other. At first, we were miracle-chasers; but, as Katie wisely points out, you can't just chase miracles. A frenzied pursuit doesn't work; miracles aren't, after all, fireflies on a warm summer evening. It has taken Katie and me years to realize what Meb knew from the beginning: our journey of the spirit is never-ending. In turn, Meb learned that it's not solely about the journey, but about enjoying the scenery along the way. We had to pool our collective resources, sometimes joking that we were like the boat at sea carrying the butcher (that would be me—adapting to the grisly task at hand), the baker (that would be Katie—cook it, eat it, and run it off tomorrow), and the candlestick-maker (that would be Meb and her vision of lighting the world), with our various skills and agendas.

We agreed from the very beginning that we would be open with each other, honest in a way that went far beyond simple "yes" or "no" answers. Meb, Katie, and I had to trust each other, knowing that once we were vulnerable we wouldn't be abandoned, laughed at (well, maybe just a little), or criticized. We made each other think more, probing each other for life facts, tidbits, and hints about inner thoughts and dream lives. We had to share parts of ourselves that we didn't necessarily want to expose—some that we didn't even know existed. Somewhere along the way, this openness allowed our lives to become intertwined in such a way that instead of keeping miracles at arm's-length, we embraced and absorbed the miraculous as part of our being.

We had spent so much time thinking about miracles, the different types that occur, where they happen, and the people they touch, that at one point—much to Meb and Katie's amusement—I came up with the concept of a miracle pyramid. I thought it would be a perfect visual for describing the organization of miracles. (And "Why shouldn't miracles be organized?" I asked a skeptical Meb and Katie.) With thunderbolts at the rarefied top (to make Katie happy) and random acts of coincidence at the expansive base (to make Meb proud), I envisioned some immense space/time continuum where miracles could ultimately all be explained. I became engrossed with the whole pyramid thing—think *Raiders of the Lost Ark* meets Joan of Arc—initiating conversations about the dollar bill and Nicholas Cage movies, not to mention prophecy and historical commentary.

"Okay, Joan, you've lost your mind," Meb declared.

"Hand over your library cards," Katie demanded.

I laughed, realizing that while chasing miracles had awakened a different relationship with God, the Miracle Chase had awakened a wonderful new relationship with each other. Our miracle meetings had set a tone of generosity of spirit that I had been worried I would miss when I could no longer be at our meetings in person; but over the years, our bond became stronger as the ideas we discussed and the time we spent commiserating over issues in our daily lives drew us closer as friends.

It was a good thing, because when I called Meb and Katie on New Year's morning 2009 from Colorado with one more story, they were willing to listen, even though it was early.

"Joan," Katie interrupted, "I just saw on TV that there was a bomb scare in Aspen and there really were bombs and the guy killed himself a ways up Independence Pass."

"What!" shouted Meb. "Are you guys okay?"

"Yeah. It was pretty weird, though. A block away from us, downtown Aspen was completely evacuated. Some guy was pretty upset with the local politicians, but no one else got hurt—just him. But that's not what I called to tell you. I have an amazing story for you."

"Wait—more amazing than a mad bomber closing down Aspen on New Year's Eve!?" Katie was incredulous.

"You decide, but let me tell you the story. Last night we had this family over for appetizers before dinner. Gene and Greg had met them while skiing on the back of Aspen Mountain the other day. Alex, the dad, is this intense cardiothoracic surgeon from L.A. The mom seemed nice, she's from Holland, and they came over with their two children."

"Joan, the point, please. I want to go back to bed. It is New Year's Day, for God's sake," Meb reminded me.

"Okay, so Alex starts telling us this story about what had happened on Christmas Eve. It was a blizzard here and he and Nick, his fourteen-year-old son, were out skiing on Ajax Mountain. Alex explained that they had a guide with them, because they had never been to Aspen before. They had also taken walkie-talkies so they could talk to each other in case they got separated in the bad weather. While they were on one of the steep trails, skiing through the trees, Nick stopped to catch his breath—parts of the mountain are over ten thousand feet, you know," I told Meb and Katie.

"Go on. . . ." Meb encouraged.

"According to Alex, by the time Nick radioed that he had stopped, Alex and the guide were already farther down the mountain. Alex told his son to ski down, 'Right now!' Even for a guy with nerves of steel, Alex was nervous because he had lost sight of his son in the whiteout conditions.

"Now Nick, who up until then in this conversation hadn't said a word, except a muffled hello when he first came inside, spoke up. 'I thought I saw something under one of the trees. But Dad was yelling at me, telling me to come down the mountain. Instead of going, though, I tried to get closer to what I thought I saw. I wiped off my goggles to try and see better; it was snowing really hard and tough to see.' He paused, taking a big breath before continuing. 'As I got closer, out of all the whiteness around me, there was a little something purple. I told Dad. He said forget it, just a scrap, ski down. Now. But I had to see what it was. As I got closer, I had to bend down, and when I touched it, I realized it was a part of a snowboard. 'Dad,' I yelled, 'that thing I saw is part of a snowboard.' 'Come down,' came my father's voice, echoed by the guide. But I started digging. 'Dad,' I said, 'there's a boot attached to the snowboard.' I heard the guide curse in the background. Dad told me they were coming up and to keep talking—so they could find me.'

"Nick dug some more and some more and you guys, you're not going to believe this, but attached to the ski boot was a fifteen-year-old girl, dressed all in white, upside down, stuck in the tree-well."

"Oh my God," Katie exclaimed.

"Now Alex took the story-telling back over, his son clearly overwhelmed by the circumstances as well as by the telling.

"He described how he knocked on her ski helmet a few times with his pole, to see if she was alive, but she was out cold. They carefully dug her out and laid her down, covering her with his new parka—he laughed, pointing to the bright orange coat I had hung up shortly before. When she awoke, she had no idea of what had happened. She didn't seem to have anything broken, but clearly was shaken up and cold. They stayed with her and kept her talking for nearly an hour until the ski patrol could find them and take her down the mountain. By then, Alex told us, 'I was nearly frozen and was really happy to get my coat back.'"

Meb and Katie were completely silent, so I continued.

"Alex said, 'The story was in the Aspen paper today and tomorrow we are going to meet the girl's family. Hey, how cool would it be,' he theorized, 'if, say, twenty years from now these two get married and

Nick can tell the kids he found their mother like a present under a tree on Christmas Eve?'"

Together, the three of us laughed in our now familiar way.

"Gene told me later, 'That's a real miracle—that girl could have been there until spring. Those trees are so close together and there's so much snow right now. It's a record snow year. No one ever would have found her—even once they started looking.'

"And that, my friends," I summed up the story, "is how miracles of coincidence happen. Remember when I told you I'd read 'a coincidence is God's way of performing a miracle anonymously'? Well, miracles are also God's way of connecting the dots. What a great way to start the New Year."

Ever since our fateful morning together in the coffee shop when I'd had to answer "I don't know" to the seemingly simple question posed by Katie and Meb, the implications of miracles of coincidence had been gnawing at me. I could now answer the question much more clearly, recognizing how the ripple of a miracle continues to arc ever outward, continuing onward into the present. The Aspen story provided an example of divine providence that could be explained by human intervention or mere coincidence. But unlike the Deists—who included America's founding fathers, Benjamin Franklin, George Washington, and Thomas Jefferson— and their belief system that removed anything supernatural from the notion of God, I believe in something more. The miracle definition that Meb, Katie, and I came up with celebrates this personal interface with God that we all felt in the extraordinary events we experienced. In light of the miracle-ee discussion we had with each other, I wondered how this young woman's experience of survival will affect her life.

Meb kept telling me it was my job to write about coincidences and miracles. Coincidences were everywhere, but at what point do they become miracles? Procrastinating one morning before I sat down to write (yes, even Energizer Bunnies procrastinate), I had turned to the newspaper for an update on world events and was captivated by what I saw. The front-page story started simply enough as a tale of Iraq, soldiers, and warfare, but soon transitioned to a human-interest story about a Marine who, while searching a house for hostile fire, instead found a baby needing assistance. This child wasn't a casualty of the war; she was a casualty of the uncertainty of life, having been born with a rare and dangerous condition where her abdominal organs had grown externally.

The child was called Mariam—another name, an ancient name, for Mary. She became the cause célèbre for a group of committed Marines. They pleaded for the child's treatment and transfer back to the United States. While a hospital had been found to underwrite Mariam's surgery and businesses had come forward to cover the costs of her transportation, progress stagnated in the military bureaucracy generated by the thousands of Iraqis who were seeking medical care.

As time dwindled before their unit left Iraq and with no rescue date for the child in sight, the physician who had been the initial contact went to the chaplain for advice. Reminiscent of Father Declan in the church parking lot that day with me, the priest asked simply whether he had prayed; the physician answered honestly that he had not. The priest suggested the Memorare ". . . never was it known that anyone who fled to thy protection, implored your help or sought your intercession, was left unaided . . ." The very next morning, after the Marine physician uttered these powerful words, the e-mail authorizing Mariam's travel to the U.S. was received. The newspaper called it "An Act of God" and quoted those involved as saying "There were too many coincidences for it to be coincidence." When I told Meb the story, she was skeptical, noting the potential for wartime propaganda, but still she appreciated how another family had been impacted by the same compelling plea to Mary that had sustained her in her own Night of Fire in the hospital room so many years ago.

One twentieth-century philosopher described miracles as "the recreating and deepening of that order in the face of all that threatens to break it down through sin, disease, violence, death, or evil of any kind." Like Mariam, we have faced evil, violence, and disease; and like the girl in the Colorado story, a series of events conspired to create a different existence than might otherwise have resulted. I've been reassured in this view of God's involvement in daily life. It's a new way of thinking, a jump shift.

We spoke about this at one of our last miracle meetings. As usual, I wanted to multi-task and put our miracle discussion into a context whereby other mysteries could also be explained.

"Did you guys know I studied gerontology back in graduate school?" I asked.

"Wait a minute. When you were in grad school, that wasn't one of the options," Meb replied seriously.

"You know how it is, Meb: I wanted to work with terminally ill children, but then I realized you had to take the whole family along as well—siblings, parents, grandparents. A sick child impacts the whole family. The study of aging was a natural for me, and it was just beginning to evolve.

"Think about it," I continued. "The evolution of miracles is like the aging process. Remember when we were young? Stories made us happy or sad—we just took everything that we were told at face value. Sometimes we asked 'why,' but we could be generally satis-fied with a simple 'because I said so.' We instantly accepted what we were told because we trusted people to tell us the truth. That's how I think people in early times thought about miracles: the 'elders' or the 'church' said it 'was,' and so 'it was'."

Katie interjected: "So you mean, by the time of the Enlighten-ment, people were waking up, becoming more like adults and for the first time asking questions?"

"Exactly. But you know what the good thing is?" I asked. Before I could answer my own rhetorical question, Meb was all over it.

"Yeah, now it's like we've entered older adulthood and we've been given permission to speak out more clearly, accepting what we want and able to reject the rest."

I laughed at our now-seamless efforts to make a connection. "This reminds me of my ninety-year-old very Italian grandmother. She didn't know very much English, but at every occasion, and much as my parents would give her the evil eye, she always bugged me about getting married—she feared at age twenty-five I was a spinster already. At her age, being diplomatic was no longer important—she was finally free to think and to say what she wanted."

I knew we had made it this far in our miracle chase because we had gone outside the box, and in so doing we had gained the courage to believe in our dreams. We had come to accept that which was beyond our reality and lay within our hearts. It was a good feeling.

Our individual transformations are well under way. While our experiences changed us, we found out that running away doesn't make a miracle any less real. The new Katie says, firmly, "All miracles require that we suspend disbelief, if only for a moment, but it is in that moment that we may just find the secret of life." She now knows that a miracle speaks to the presence and the power of God. And the newly practical-minded Meb explained that the whole conversation on miracles would have been different if translated through her-story instead of his-story. While the Wise Guys spent too much time trying to define, prove, or disprove the existence of miracles, we wise women simply appreciated them enough to want to pass them along.

Not so long ago, I picked up a small, funky plaque in my kitchen and wondered why I even had this seemingly homemade piece of kitsch. As I looked closer, it was a montage of Our Lady of Fatima and the children who saw her. I thought perhaps that it was like my old torn flags or palm fronds from past years' celebrations—that is, until I turned it over. On the back was an autograph from my dad. One of only three things I own from the seventy-seven years he lived that he inscribed himself, having left most of the signing to someone else. I'm sure it was his way of sending along a greeting from a European trip he was taking with my mother. At the time, I lived thousands of miles away and was pregnant with his first grandchild, and I know he would have worried about both of us. His wording was wistful. He had written a short dedication: "To Joan, Gene and Friend, Fatima, May, 1984. Blessings, Dad." Funny how Fatima showed up on my doorstep: a portent of the future. For it was to Mary that I turned for help as a mother in my moment of need. Was my father prescient about protecting his number one grandson when he could no longer do so himself on earth?

Actually, my father had a lot in common with C. S. Lewis. Both were Anglophiles: Lewis by birth, my dad a veteran of the Army Air Force in WWII in London; both were writers: one successful, writing for the masses, one less so, writing for family and friends; both were down to earth, religious, though practical in their approach. I could see my dad sitting me down and uttering Lewis's words telling me that miracles "are precisely those chapters in this great story on which the plot turns . . . and had we but eyes to see it, this has been hinted on every page, met us, in some disguise, at every turn, and even been uttered in conversations . . . but it is a very long story, with a complicated plot, and we are not, perhaps, very attentive listeners." On that last part, Dad would be looking straight into my eyes, his lawyer's glance sensing my guilt at moving too quickly, not hearing or listening to the whole message, whatever it was.

So a few years ago, when planning a family trip to Greece and Turkey, I set out with a goal to learn, to take notice, to listen, so that the spirit of the lands we would visit would speak to me. This was my pilgrimage to a holy place, the destination to which my Miracle Chase had led me. Given our itinerary, exploring the ruins of the early Christian Church was inevitable. And so, after walking in the footsteps of Julius Caesar, Mark Antony, and Cleopatra, we walked the land of St. Paul and the area of Ephesus where John and Mary had once lived. Maryisma, outside of Ephesus, is believed to be the last place Mary lived on earth. Just the thought of visiting her home was daunting to me.

The site is beautiful, set high on a hill, once with a view of the sea, protected and protectable. It is a peaceful place, a natural stream flowing between the lush pine trees, inviting and tranquil in spite of the hordes of visitors. Some days it is quiet here. However, the day we visit is a busy one and some foreign head of state, complete with bodyguards and medical staff, reminds us that we must face the practicality of our day even while paying homage to those who lived so long ago.

Upon passing under the doorway to the understated stone enclosure, which was once Mary's home and now houses a chapel, I am enveloped by the presence of warmth and respect. We are ushered in by a friar and supposed to pass through single-file, without stopping, leaving as unobtrusively as possible. This I can not do. As my family moves along, I find a small corner in which to contemplate all that has happened over the past ten years. Tears of gratitude well up as I realize the gifts we have been given and the protection we have been offered.

So many children die of abuse, and yet Elizabeth awoke from her coma to become a beacon of hope and a poster child for the resilience of the human spirit. Katie met a serial killer head on, looked him straight in the eye, and was saved. Jim, with a 99% blockage in the "widow maker" artery, missed a dream trip to Europe but dodged a deadly bullet for high-stress, white-collar males, especially those unlucky ones with a family history of heart disease. David should have been dead but isn't, and instead after a successful college swimming career is now pursuing a calling in medicine. And me—instead of the death sentence I anticipated, with a large cancerous growth inside my chest, I got a reprieve, the opportunity to be here and now, grateful for all that we have experienced and survived.

As I stand in the chapel, not wanting to leave, I understand that I merely need to accede to the miraculous, to accept and be grateful for the gifts I have been given. As I walk out of the chapel, I am greeted by Gregory, my child who had once loved the white rainbows in the sky as much as the colorful ones. He is standing and looking at the wall of intentions that had been left by other pilgrims to Maryisma. Greg asks if we can leave the red bracelet he has worn since April commemorating the life of his classmate's sister, so that Mary could intercede and care for her. Lovingly, we wrap the bracelet, write a note, and attach it to the wall. The parallels are not lost on any of us as we carefully acknowledge her life with God while rejoicing in our family life here together on earth.

Having faced death, and having had the opportunity to recognize life for the gift it is, is perhaps the greatest miracle to me. It makes Pascal's wager as poignant today as it was to him in his conversion—for in believing a little, we get a lot. I am finally able to admit that God was really speaking to me that January day in the hospital waiting room and that my family was singled out for divine providence. I understand that a miracle happened in my life. Hearing my name, "Luise," coming from the television might just as well have been the voice of God, and I knew in my heart that all would be well. I wasn't consciously looking for a sign or even a miracle, but the peace that came over me, at that moment, vanquished my once-cavalier perspective forever. I now am willing to recognize the hand of God, where before I would have just smiled agreeably, the Cheshire cat of miracle lore.

As I closed the lid on Pandora's box, I discovered from the beginning that it was all about miracles; and in the end, it is as well. The Miracle Chase had not been my dream of a lifetime or a burning issue smoldering within my consciousness for years, but it became my passion—the pursuit of a new spirituality—empowering me to dispel the cynicism of my life and embrace the challenge of becoming better.

Oh, and remember that plant Meb pruned ten years ago? Well, it is alive and thriving in my guest room, where Katie and Meb are always welcome visitors. Like the plant, the three of us nurtured our own growth, cutting back the dead weight and allowing new shoots to take root and flourish.

It took the firm resolve of Meb trusting her instincts to trim that plant and let it live—her steadfast determination will keep her whole. Katie, too, has found her way to the sun, pulling out the weeds along the way that held her back. As for me, with the support of my amazing miracle friends, I am able at long last to unwind the ties that restricted my thinking, finally twirling them round and round like streamers spiraling ever longer and longer until they burst apart.

MIRACLE WORKS FOUNDATION

The meaning of life is to find your gift,
The purpose of life is to give it away.

—Joy J. Golliver

As "gifts freely bestowed," our personal miracles have engendered in us a belief that the miracles in our lives should be shared with others. This "unfolding and beneficial connection between the Divine and humankind" has inspired us to form the **MiracleWorks Foundation**. We are passionate about the potential for women to advance their own personal status as a means to improve the well-being of their families and communities. The **MiracleWorks Foundation** is part of our ongoing Ripple Effect and we are called to make it happen.

The **MiracleWorks Foundation** is devoted to improving the future for women and children who are educationally and economically disadvantaged, survivors of domestic and international violence, or victims of child abuse and neglect. The **MiracleWorks Foundation** is deeply committed to identifying, understanding and impacting programs that strengthen these vulnerable constituencies through advancing health, education and safety as well as fostering opportunities for economic independence.

Together, we have over sixty years of combined experience managing, expanding, and enhancing programs in nonprofit organizations focused on women's health, disability rights, and the education and rights of the child. As experienced leaders, we are committed to providing financial and technical assistance in support of the mission of the **MiracleWorks Foundation**. The nonprofit **MiracleWorks**

Foundation is funded through a portion of the proceeds from the book, *The Miracle Chase*, as well as support from private donors, foundations, and trusts. For more information please go to http://www.TheMiracleChase.com

BIBLIOGRAPHY

Alexander, Caroline, *The Endurance: Shackleton's Legendary Antarctic Expedition*. Knopf, 2000.

Appelbaum, David, ed., "Miracles," *Parabola*, Winter 1997, Volume XXII, No. 4. Society for the Study of Myth and Tradition, New York.

Armstrong, Karen, *A History of God: The 4,000-Year Quest of Judaism, Christianity and Islam*. Ballantine, 1993.

Augustine, translated by F. J. Sheed, *Confessions*. Hackett Publishing, 2006.

Beck, Martha, *Expecting Adam: A True Story of Birth, Rebirth, and Everyday Magic*. Crown, 1999.

Bierhorst, John, *The Mythology of North American Indians*. Oxford University Press, 2002.

Blunt, Wilfrid S., *The Future of Islam*. London, 1882.

Brown, Colin, *Miracles and the Critical Mind*. Eerdmans, 1984.

Burnham, Sophy, *A Book of Angels*. Ballantine, 1990.

Caduto, Michael, and Joseph Bruchac, *Native American Stories*. Fulcrum, 1981.

Cahill, Susan, ed., *Wise Women*. Norton, 1996.

Carrel, Alexis, *Journey To Lourdes*. Harper, 1950.

Campbell, Joseph, *The Hero with a Thousand Faces*. Bollingen Series, Princeton University Press, 1949.

Cole, K. C., *First You Build a Cloud and Other Reflections on Physics as a Way of Life*. Harcourt Brace, 1999.

Geisler, Norman, *Miracles and Modern Thought*. Christian Free University Curriculum, 1982.

Ghanananda, Swami, and Sir John Stewart-Wallace, editorial advisors, *Woman Saints of East and West*. Vendanta Press, 1955.

Gibbon, Edward, *Decline and Fall of the Roman Empire*. New York, 1932.

Harvey, Andrew, *Essential Mystics*. BookSales, 1998.

Hawking, Stephen, *A Brief History of Time*. Bantam, 1998.

Hood, Ann, "In Search of Miracles", Zaleski, P., ed., Best Spiritual Writing 2000, 2000.

James, Montague R., *Apocryphal New Testament*. Oxford at the Clarendon Press, 1929.

Jastrow, Robert, *God and the Astronomers*. W. W. Norton, 1978.

Kornfield, Jack, *After the Ecstasy the Laundry*. Bantam, 2001.

———, *The Wise Heart*. Bantam, 2008.

Lewis, C. S., *Miracles, A Preliminary Study*. Macmillan, 1947.

Millman, Dan, and Doug Childers, *Divine Interventions*. Daybreak Books, 1999.

Monden, Louis, *Signs and Wonders: A Study of the Miraculous Element in Religion*. Desclee, 1996.

Moore, Thomas, *Dark Nights of the Soul: A Guide to Finding Your Way Through Life's Ordeal*. Gotham Books, 2004.

Mullin, Robert, *Miracles and the Modern Religious Imagination*. Yale University Press, 1996.

Pearmain, Elisa Davy, ed., *Doorways to the Soul*. Pilgrim Press, 1998.

Pelletier, Joseph A., *The Sun Danced at Fatima*. Image Books, 1983.

Radhakrishnam, Sarvepalli, and Charles A. Moore, *A Sourcebook of Indian Philosophy*. Princeton University Press, 1957.

Sahakian, William, *History of Philosophy*. Barnes & Noble, 1968.

Smith, Huston, *The World's Religions*. Harper San Francisco, 1991.

———, *Why Religion Matters*. Harper San Francisco, 2001.

Swamp, Chief Jake, *The Peacemaker's Journey*, Parabola Audio, 1996.

———, *The Peacemakers*, "Peace," Parabola, Fall, 1996. Volume XXI, No. 3, Society for the Study of Myth and Tradition, New York.

Van den Beukel, A., *More Things in Heaven and Earth*. SCM Press, 1991.

Wallace, Paul A. W., *The Iroquois Book of Life—White Roots of Peace*. Clear Light, 1994.

Werfel, Franz, *The Song of Bernadette*, St. Martin's Press, 1942.

Woodward, Kenneth, *Making Saints*. Simon & Schuster, 1990.

———, *The Book of Miracles*. Simon & Schuster, 2000.

ACKNOWLEDGMENTS

The authors would like to acknowledge and thank the following people for their vision and support:

Michael Fragnito for his willingness to believe in miracles and see the spark of possibilities in a short query letter sent by three unknown authors;

Kate Zimmermann, our editor, for her help in bringing our miracle dream to life;

Our families for loving us and our parents for giving us the tools to find our voices and the freedom to follow our dreams;

Eric Vormanns, Msgr. Paul Garrity, and Fr. Declan Deane, for encouraging us in our own spiritual journeys;

Artie Boyle, Mary Jensen, Tony Di Croce, Laura Epstein Flink, Lei Anne Ellis, the Faulkner family, Julie and Woody Tausend, Guide Dogs for the Blind, Jennifer Wines, Maryanne Comaroto, the Stapleton family, and others for the privilege of hearing and sharing their stories;

Liz Phillips, Maureen Mahon Egen, Pat Mahon, Paula Morgan, and Jack Coyne for their inspiration and encouragement;

Richard Galton, Doe Coover, the Moraga Book Group, the Prides-Farm Girls Club, and our friends for listening, reading, and believing;

And all the Wise Guys and Wonder Women for paving the way before us.

ABOUT THE AUTHORS

Joan, Katie, and Meb, New Year's Eve 1999

JOAN LUISE HILL has spent over twenty-five years in the health-care industry. Her numerous community volunteer jobs include her ten-year tenure as president of the Foundation for Osteoporosis Research and Education (FORE), a nonprofit organization dedicated to increasing awareness and prevention of osteoporosis through education, testing, and research. Under her leadership, FORE sponsored key osteoporosis legislation in California and turned a nearly bankrupt organization into one of the nation's leading osteoporosis centers. Currently, Joan serves on the board of trustees of St. Mary's High School in Lynn, Massachusetts, an inner-city Catholic school and as a member of the Council of Women at Boston College. She has a Master's degree from the University of Connecticut and a Bachelor of Science degree from Boston College. After returning to live for nine years in a suburb of Boston with her husband, Gene, and three children, Joan and family have returned to California, where her youngest child, Gregory, is in high school; her daughter, Alyssa, has graduated from Georgetown University and is currently attending law school; and her oldest, David, has graduated from Colgate University and works in medical research.

KATIE MAHON, a banker for seventeen years, retired in 1997 to stay at home full-time with her daughters while also continuing her focus on nonprofit initiatives that support women's health and quality education for children. She is a three-time past president of the San Francisco Susan G. Komen Breast Cancer Foundation, an organization that Katie helped take from a grassroots movement to a million-dollar organization reaching thousands in need across the Bay Area. She also served for five years on the board of The College Preparatory School (College Prep) in Oakland, California where she focused on the school's financial aid goals. She holds a Bachelor of Science degree in Psychology from the University of Santa Clara and attended graduate school in Business at Golden Gate University in San Francisco. Katie now lives in New York City with her husband, Jim. She is the mother of two daughters. Laura, a graduate of Harvard University, and Allie, a graduate of Tufts University in 2010, are both working in New York City.

MARY BETH PHILLIPS (Meb) has been an advocate for children and families since her six-month-old baby daughter was severely shaken by a neighbor's nanny and permanently blinded. Outraged by how little the criminal-justice system valued children, Meb's career took a sharp turn from that of a dean in higher education to that of an advocate for child protection and quality childcare. Meb was the "mother" of the ground-breaking California Trustline Registry, legislation that impacted child care in California and the nation. Over the years, she has been a therapist, an organizational consultant and a garden designer. Currently, as the executive director for a nonprofit organization, Meb provides technical assistance and support for centers that work with families who have children with special needs. Meb holds a Bachelor of Science and a Master's degree in Marriage and Family Counseling from the University of Santa Clara, and a PhD in Clinical Psychology from the California School of Professional Psychology. She has three children: Liz, a graduate of Stanford University currently at the University of Arizona at Tucson in a PhD program in Philosophy; Andrew, a graduate of the University of California at Davis, currently teaching students with emotional disabilities; and Daniel, an author, singer and songwriter, who is living and going to school in Boston.

Reading Group Guide

1. In the beginning of the book, how do the three friends differ from one another in their thinking about miracles? Are their views colored by their own experiences? How do their opinions change over time?

2. Of the three authors, is there one that you particularly identify with?

3. How did the Miracle Chase enhance the developing friendship between the three authors? What qualities and characteristics did the authors need to cultivate in order to be able to continue their miracle search both on an individual level and as part of a team?

4. Were there historical facts or religious concepts in the book that surprised you? Did you gain any insights about other religions? How did the book make you feel about your own spiritual choices?

5. Eric Vormanns, the shaman and healer, refers to the "one true God." What does it mean to believe in the one true God?

6. The authors become intrigued by Augustine and his mother. Are there circumstances today where the behavior of mothers like Monica—the ultimate helicopter parent—is acceptable?

7. When Katie's husband experiences a medical crisis, she questions the role of prayer and faith. How do the personal crises the women face affect their Miracle Chase?

8. Joan gets spooked by the "Death by Miracle" theme first, and then all three become wary later on. Is this just silly superstition, or something more? Did it affect the Chase?

9. Meb prayed for a miracle to save her marriage. Does praying for a miracle that never comes affect one's belief in miracles? What if the miracle you get isn't the one you asked for?

10. Katie realizes that there is no complete answer to why she lived and others didn't. Joan finally believes that a miracle happened in her family and that divine intervention reaches into the ordinary. Meb sees her daughter's journey as a miracle in and of itself. What other conclusions did the authors draw in the book? How do you feel about these conclusions?

11. By the end of their Miracle Chase, the authors suggest that the most important aspect of miracles is their Ripple Effect. How do you feel about the notion of miracles extending forward into time?

12. What is your favorite miracle story from the book? Are there stories that you struggled to believe or understand?

13. Did the book encourage you to look at any of your own life experiences differently? Have you ever met someone who has experienced a miracle?

14. Do you believe in miracles?